Navy Proud

Navy Proud

Allen W. Van Osdol Jr

SG Enterprises©
Crawfordsville, Indiana

NAVY PROUD

First Edition

Photo research by: Allen W. Van Osdol Jr.

Cover design: Allen W. Van Osdol Jr.

Edited by: Allen W. Van Osdol Jr.

Printed in the United States of America

ISBN-10: 098533570X
ISBN-13: 9780985335700

Library of Congress Control Number: 2015905131

Published by SG Enterprises©
209 Aspen Drive, Suite 101
Crawfordsville, Indiana U.S.A.

Dedicated to my wonderful wife Diane

Although she wasn't aware of her influence, she caused me to think about my life while in the United States Navy, and to realize my service did make a difference. I see the pride in her eyes when she speaks about my military service and I want her to know I appreciate it.

Contents

Acknowledgements · ix

Introduction · xi

Chapter 1 Boot Camp · 1

Chapter 2 ADR School · 39

Chapter 3 Barber's Point · 55

Chapter 4 Tripler Army Hospital · · · · · · · · · · · · · · · 73

Chapter 5 Hard Lessons · 81

Chapter 6 Ford Island · 91

Chapter 7 Ream Field · 101

Chapter 8 U.S.S. Kitty Hawk · · · · · · · · · · · · · · · · · 115

Chapter 9 Subic Bay · 127

Chapter 10 Treasure Island · · · · · · · · · · · · · · · · · · · 139

Post Face · 143

Disclaimer · 145

Photo Credits · 147

Acknowledgements

I AM GRATEFUL TO ALISON Bliss, a published author of a wonderfully exciting book, Rules of Protection, for her encouragement on this project. I know she put much effort into trying to make me a good writer. I hope I live up to her high standards.

I also want to thank Tom Bigley, CDR USNR-TAR (Retired) for his generosity in allowing me to use photos from his web site, http://home. earthlink.net/~patron40.

The photos he allowed me to borrow show the same type aircraft I remember working on but didn't have the foresight to photograph myself.

I want to thank mustang, Chief Warrant Officer 4, Warren Willis, (Electronics Technician) for the pleasure of reading about his life in the Navy. A few of the photos used in this book were borrowed from his web site and credited thusly. Please take the time to view and read the below listed web site. I know you will enjoy it.

I want to express my appreciation for the executive assistance provided by my daughter Carolyn S. Van Osdol Largent on this project.

I include this photo because my sister Mary thought enough of it to save it.

Introduction

THE CONTINENTAL CONGRESS ESTABLISHED THE first organized American Navy in 1775. A young lieutenant by the name of John Paul Jones, became an officer in the newly born *National* Navy. Jones would later become an inspiration to many a Navy man. As the captain of the USS Bonhomme Richard, he told the British, "I have not yet begun to fight," after being asked to surrender. He then led his crew on to defeat the British war ship *Serapis*.

It was this attitude I felt emanating from the television programs, *Navy Log* and *Victory at Sea*. I enjoyed watching them for some time before I was old enough to join the Navy.

I knew early on that I wanted to be a sailor, and I made no distinction between an officer and an enlisted man. I just wanted to be in the Navy.

I hope all who read this, enjoy my story. It is not my intention to recite minute-by-minute or hour-by-hour occurrences but rather a loosely woven synopsis of my life and happenings during the time I served as a sailor. Some dates may not be exact but they are as close as I can remember.

I cannot speak for everyone, but I know there are many who feel as I do, regardless of his or her branch of service. This includes honor, for being allowed to serve, gratitude, for those who have gone before, and those who gave everything they could give for our country and our freedom.

There are those who are envious and even jealous of the freedoms we Americans enjoy, if not appreciate.

As long as there are true Americans willing to fight and protect our nation and our rights, from enemies from outside and from within, the un-Americans cannot win.

Our enemies have in the past and will surely again in the future, bloody our nose, but, as many who have gone before us, some will stand up and continue to fight until the *Stars and Stripes* again flies over all the *Mount Suribachi's* and twin towers of the world.

Pearl Harbor did not defeat us. The *Twin Towers* did not defeat us. Bombs and bullets will never defeat us. Only *We the People,* through our own greed, apathy and desire for immediate gratification can destroy our great nation.

The United States Navy is a proud service and I am proud to have been a small part of it.

CHAPTER 1

Boot Camp

WHO KNOWS WHY A SEVENTEEN-YEAR-OLD boy, as I had been in nineteen six-ty-two, does what he does?

I remember thinking, my father and uncles all enlisted in the Army but, I wanted to be different.

Television programs I watched whenever possible called, *Navy Log* and *Victory at Sea*, fascinated me with the many documentaries showing life aboard ship and naval battles during World War II.

Becoming a sailor and a part of the excitement and seeing the world, became a strong desire in me. As I grew older, the desire grew as well until I turned seventeen, then I thought I was a man and could make my own decisions and I decided to join the United States Navy; as soon as Mom and Dad gave me permission.

In August 1962, I convinced my parents to give consent and sign for me to go into the Navy instead of starting my junior year of high school.

After completing my sophomore year by the skin of my teeth, I didn't want to go back to school. High school became quite boring for me, and I wasn't interested in sports because I didn't do well at any of them.

Mom and Dad tried to dissuade me from quitting school but I stuck to my adult guns. Only I knew the best route for me.

When I joined, I received a choice of going to boot camp in either the Great Lakes or San Diego. I felt the need to get as far from home and cold weather as I could so I chose sunny cali-forn-ia.

My Uncle Glenn lived in California and I thought maybe I would get a chance to see him. I did get to visit him but not for two or three years.

I went home for the night after the swearing in ceremony at the recruiting office. I also received the most complete physical ever in my life. I don't think any area of me hadn't been touched.

I talked with Mom and Pop, telling them of my day's experiences. I said my goodbyes to my little brothers and sisters and tried to comfort the ones with tears in their eyes.

Early the next morning a recruiter, in a gray Navy car, picked me and then a couple of other guys up at our homes. We each brought a small suitcase with essentials.

The recruiter took us back to the office in Indianapolis where we waited, for several hours, before boarding a bus that took us to Weircook Airport on the west side of Indianapolis.

Flying both excited me and scared me a bit having never been on an airplane before.

When the plane took off and left the ground, I felt such an adrenalin rush, I didn't want to land. I looked out the window the entire flight, seeing the land falling away and cars and houses getting smaller.

I loved looking at the clouds from the top side for several hours, getting glimpses of the earth and all the tiny, quite indistinguishable things below. I enjoyed the flight with plenty of time to think about what the future held for me.

Undoubtedly, I wanted to do the best thing for me, which also confirmed in my mind, my adulthood.

I could see the houses, and roads, while they grew larger as we descended getting ready to land.

At the airport a Navy Chief met us and directed us to get on a waiting, navy, gray bus. I, along with a group of other young guys, arrived at RTC, *Recruit Training Center,* receiving unit, San Diego, California, in the late afternoon.

Someone showed us where to stow our gear and sleep for the night. The old barracks smelled musty but I guess it didn't matter because we only stayed one night.

The afternoon we arrived many of the guys in uniform yelled at the kids who just got there. They barked orders, go here, go there, stand at attention and do this or that. It seemed like total chaos, sometimes not even knowing who to listen to.

At only seventeen I thought I knew everything. Among a good many other people, most didn't seem to know any more than I did. To me, anyone wearing a uniform had to be special, with the authority of an admiral.

⬿∾

Our first full day began before daylight or 0 dark thirty, the sailor who woke us, beating on a trash can, told us.

We formed a line, asshole to belly button as the order came down, whenever we stood in line the first few days, like when we waited to get our haircuts or go to chow.

I don't know why but somebody wanted the line to look as short as possible. Talk about close ranks!

Outside the receiving barracks on the pavement, freshly painted squares about two feet or so square with a number in each box. We had to stand in a square and remember the number. The rest of the day, if we weren't lined up to do something, we stood in our numbered boxes.

If memory serves me, a big part of the first and second day we spent filling out paperwork, which I learned there is no lack of in the military. In time, I would learn there were forms to fill out to get other forms in all branches of the service.

Groups of us went somewhere, filled out some papers, and returned to our numbered boxes and waited for the next order to do something.

The first few days passed by fast due to our busy schedule.

We received instructions to read everything we signed. The amount of paperwork we read and signed became overwhelming.

A lot of the forms asked for the same information as previous forms but for a different reason.

Our uniforms were issued, unbeknownst to me, the cost would be deducted from our pay.

We got our shots and haircuts (all the way to the scalp), which took less than twenty seconds each.

There wasn't time for relaxing in those barber chairs. Woe be unto the poor guy who didn't tell the barber about the mole on his head which included me.

We marched a hundred miles or more and stood in line, waiting, for twenty hours each day, which is a long time to be packed like sardines. Hurry up and wait is the military way.

We received our service numbers and told to memorize them. I never forgot mine. The numbers back then, weren't like now, where they just use the person's Social Security number.

If you ask any veteran in before the mid-seventies, I bet he/she will remember their service number.

It seemed like we spent hours stenciling our names, service numbers or initials on each piece of clothing with either white ink on a white stencil brush on dark items or with black ink on a black brush on white things. Stencils could only be in specific locations on everything.

We held up each article the instructor told us to hold, until everyone held the same thing in his hands, the same as when we inventoried our sea bags to make sure we all had everything we were supposed to.

I felt like an idiot holding up six pairs of skivvies, six pairs of black socks, one white web belt, or one black web belt and so on. Finding all of each item, and waiting for everyone else to find his, seemed to take forever.

The instructor explained how to lay each piece on the table and how to place the stencil.

Place the correct stencil in the correct position on the correct article; dab the correct brush on the correct inkpad; then brush back and forth across the stencil until the ink became clear on the item. Repeat several hundred times until everything in your sea bag bore your stencil.

Several sailors walked around checking and correcting us if the item wasn't positioned right or if the stencil was in the wrong place. Seemingly, stenciling took hours to complete, on the long rows of wooden tables.

The civilian clothes we wore and brought to boot camp with us, we either donated to charity or sent home, at our own expense. I didn't bring any money so mine went into the donation bin.

At home our clothes were handed down as we out grew them and I wondered what my Mom would say if she knew I just gave my clothes away.

When a sufficient number of recruits processed through all the administrative things we became a company. A Company Commander took charge of us. All of the CC's I later learned must be enlisted NCOs, either E-6 or above. Ours turned out to be an E-6.

We each slung our sea bag over our shoulder and we marched to our new barracks in Camp Nimitz. What none of us knew, our recruiters must have forgotten to tell us, the nine-and-a-half weeks of basic didn't start until after our four weeks at Camp Nimitz.

Our first real training came when we learned how to wear each part of our uniforms.

I mean everything, from plain white boxer shorts, which I hadn't worn before and I found to be most uncomfortable (I grew up wearing tighty whities), to the bell bottom trousers with thirteen buttons.

A new type of shirt to me, called a jumper, with a flap on the back called a tar flap (I have no idea why), and the leggings.

Yes, the leggings, those wonderful, uncomfortable, torture devices that served no purpose.

Learning how to fold your trouser leg and put your leggings on became an experience.

Made of canvas with laces up the outside of each leg, they fit snugly around your calf and ankle and over the tops of your Boon Dockers (high top work shoes). They felt like tightly wrapped elastic bandages. After three months, a body got used to them.

I don't think any of us knew the leggings were only for recruits, until halfway through basic training. I guess some units wore them during World War II. Their use has now been discontinued except for special occasions and boot camp for the most part.

I remember the first time I dressed in the white uniform. I was only one of many, who looked the same as me, but I was proud to be wearing the uniform.

Learning how to fold all the clothing wasn't hard. It amazed me how some people found folding clothes difficult.

My mother taught us kids, from an early age, how to fold clothes. The Navy way may be a little different, a lot of things folded in-side out, but the basics are the same.

Most of the guys in our company tried to help those having trouble with one thing or another, how to fold something the proper way or how to stow things in the small lockers. Everything we did needed to be done in a specific way.

Those who picked things up fast helped the slower learning ones. Sometimes the teachers became the students and vice versa.

The same helpfulness carried over to the military exercises (marching and maneuvers) we did on the parade grounds. Most of us learned teamwork made Boot Camp a little easier.

H.R. Jordan, ADR 1 was our Company Commander (CC) an Aviation Machinist Mate First Class.

His arm patch looked so cool with a winged propeller. I wanted to wear the same insignia also. After I found out the meaning, I applied to the aircraft mechanic school when the opportunity came.

The man, gruff and loud as he could be, put the fear of God in all of us. I don't think a single man in our company didn't hate him by graduation day, although the last week or so he didn't yell as much and only once in a while. I got the sense he was truly proud of us.

We met again several years later. I found out he wasn't such a bad guy, but in boot camp, he was a mean SOB. I never did hear him speak in a normal tone of voice.

At the time, I didn't think the man knew how to talk without yelling. The little bit my Dad yelled at me as a kid was nothing compared to this man.

A couple of years after basic training, Jordan and I would be stationed at Barber's Point Naval Air Station (BPNAS) in Hawaii and even assigned to the same barracks. Although being an E-6 he had a private room as a ranking N.C.O. (noncommissioned officer) instead of in a dorm like me.

I heard he had been stationed at BPNAS so I looked him up and we talked.

He had been in the Navy about twelve or fifteen years and now considering getting out instead of staying a few more years and retiring.

After talking and getting to know a little more about him I realized he was a pretty heavy drinker. At the time I wasn't old enough to drink and we sort of drifted apart. I don't know if he stayed in or if he went ahead and got out of the Navy.

After boot camp but before I met him in Hawaii, I found out the CC's for the Navy and D.I.'s for the Marines and Army, were taught to be hard. To yell at their recruits to teach them discipline and see who could take the pressure.

Many people have seen movies of Drill Instructors yelling at their men and for the most part that is the way it was back in those days.

Our CC told us once, he wasn't allowed to slap stupid recruits around anymore but there were no rules about throwing one of their shirts up against the wall and if the recruit was dumb enough to be in the shirt at the time; well, too bad.

I don't remember anyone washing out of our Company so I guess we all survived. I haven't met up with any of the fellas I went to boot with but maybe someday I will.

Our Company number was 474 and I went through RTC San Diego August through October 1962.

I realize now, many things I didn't deem important enough to note back then, I wish now I had.

Even the smallest of details would have been most helpful writing my story. A good deal of research has been needed to complete what I couldn't recall.

I've had fun researching and remembering things for my story and it has been a fair amount of work but I think it has been worth every hour spent doing it.

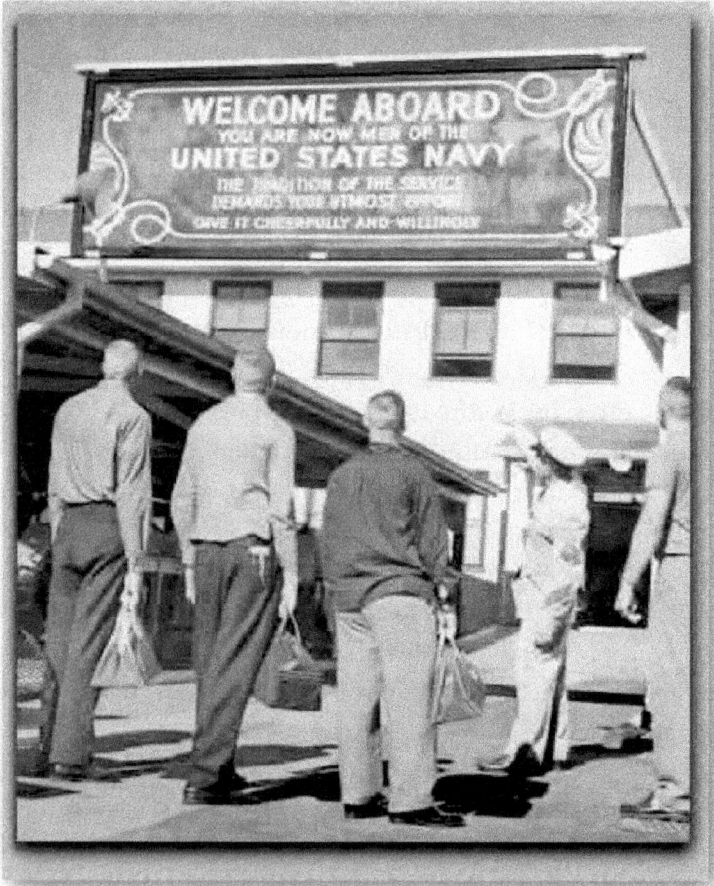

Naval Training Station, San Diego, California
Receiving Center

I remember this sign well, and reading it over and over, wanting desperately to be the best I could be. I felt proud, choosing the Navy, knowing how important it was to put forth my best effort, cheerfully and willingly, like so many sailors before me.

Nobody pointed the sign out to me as in the photo above but I knew the importance of the words and I knew the United States Navy was talking directly to me. I will never forget that sign and how it made me feel; Proud! More proud than anything ever in my life.

Do I still sound like a boot? Maybe so, but I am still filled with pride for being a swab jockey and doing my duty for my country.

Camp Nimitz is where we spent the first four weeks of our training, the time most of our recruiters forgot to tell us about.

The barracks were two story buildings. Four Companies of recruits in each building, two at each end with one on the top and bottom of the "I".

In the center of the building were heads with showers, maintenance closets as well as offices and quarters for the Company Commanders.

The first couple of weeks our company commander tried, and succeeded for the most part, to make us feel stupid and unfit to be in HIS Navy. I think he wanted to see if he could break any of us.

Everything he did, I now know, was to teach us discipline which is what boot camp is all about. He attempted to teach his men (boys) to obey orders without question and instill strict discipline in each

❧

Most of the training we received at Camp Nimitz was basic, from how to wash clothes using a bucket and scrub brush, as shown in the photos on following pages.

How to hang each article of clothing to dry and how to fold every piece the Navy way.

We practiced for hours each day learning how to march and practicing many drills with a rifle. We also enjoyed several hours at various times during the day doing calisthenics on the grinder (Parade Grounds).

We still did our drills on Camp Decatur's grinder every day but most of our days now we either spent in a class room or in a class situation such as firefighting or learning how to use a gas mask in the gas chamber and such other things which required a larger space.

My mother taught me how to do laundry, sorting whites from colors, darks from both of the others. Washing whites in hot water and colors and darks in warm.

We had no washing machines, at least not at RTC (Recruit Training Center), San Diego. I heard the boot camp in the Great Lakes had them, but it was very cold there, so I didn't care.

We scrubbed our things on big stone wash tables, and quite a few people could do their laundry at once on them, washing one thing at a time.

If you stop and think about it, having our hands in soapy water and rinsing in clean water for the time it takes to do each day's laundry, we all had the cleanest dishpan hands of our lives.

It amazed me how my fingernails looked: clean! I was brought up to wash my hands before eating but I never thought about my fingernails.

Washing clothes isn't as easy as putting them in a washing machine.

A concrete wash table with a bunch of guys trying to wash and rinse their daily laundry all at the same time. Sometimes one might get something rinsed and someone else splashes soap suds all over it and you must re-rinse it again.

A bucket, a scrub brush, hot water, and Wisk in a can is what we used to clean our clothes.

The bristles of the scrub brushes were so stiff, some of our clothes wore out by the time we graduated.

Seventeen years old and only a twenty three inch waist

Standing guard: protecting the clothesline

Many a time some of our clothes needed washing again before we could wear them because of the sea gulls. I don't think the gulls had anything against anyone personally; they didn't seem to care whose clothes they dumped on.

After scrubbing and rinsing, we hung our clothes on a clothesline outside, but not with clothespins like at home.

Each item, whether a denim shirt, tee shirt, skivvies (underwear), or socks must be hung out to dry.

Dungarees, even the whites we wore a good bit of the time, all had to be tied to the line with little strings called *clothes stops*. They were to be secured in a certain uniform way.

If our clothes weren't fastened the correct way on the line, the inspector the next morning would take them off the line, throw them on the ground, and make sure they needed to be washed again.

Do you remember I said Wisk detergent in a can to do the laundry? Someone came up with the bright idea of flattening one side of the empty soap can and rubbing it on the wash table to smooth it slick and then fill the can with hot water.

The resulting tool was a hot iron to press our uniforms. The iron worked pretty well but took a lot of work to make. One had to use a rag to hold the can because of the hot water inside.

I know what an entrepreneur is but I saw firsthand how it works in boot camp. Two guys in our company made extra money by washing or ironing clothes for others as well as polishing shoes and or brass.

I'm not aware how much they charged for their services, which could not have been much, but I had no money and didn't take advantage of their offers. Several of our rank and file used them throughout our training though.

As I said before, all clothing had to be folded in a specific way and stowed in a quite small locker in a regulated way.

Little time passed before all of us learned how to stow everything as the company commander had shown us or suffer the consequences of having everything thrown on the floor during daily barracks inspection.

The only things not stowed in our lockers were our personal items such as letters and toiletries.

This included our razors, shaving cream (neither of which did I need at that time), soap, toothbrush and paste. Those all had to be kept in what we called a *ditty bag* but even that must be hung in a specific way on our rack (bed).

I don't remember anyone in our company ever getting in trouble for stealing. All of our possessions were accessible to everyone else but we encountered no problems to my knowledge.

We heard scuttlebutt of someone being caught stealing something in another company though.

We didn't have sheets on our bunks, or racks, as we called them; we used what everyone called *fart sacks*. You are free to decide for yourself how that name came to be.

A fart sack is a large white, heavy material, bag made to snuggly fit over a military mattress, just like a pillowcase. The open end had tie strings attached, and they had to be tied in a specific way to secure the fart sack on the mattress.

The mattresses issued to us seemed quite a bit thinner than even the least expensive mattress a civilian can buy now. The ties of the fart sack were either on the top side or on the bottom side if the mattress was turned over.

I don't remember which side should be up to sleep on, but we had to turn the mattress over in the morning and then turn it back over at night to sleep on.

Our blanket had to be regulation folded and positioned in the correct spot at the foot of the mattress during the day as well.

This turned out to be one more thing used to teach discipline, and believe me, many of us got gigged during inspection the first couple of days for not turning our mattress over in the morning.

This meant we had to wash our fart sacks again before we put them back on the mattress. The Company Commander made sure it became too dirty to sleep on.

Scrubbing a fart sack turned out to be a most difficult task, and you did not want to do it more than necessary.

Learning military time did not come easy, at least for me. The first twelve hours is not hard, but after that, it's more difficult.

I still need to think about converting the time sometimes if I want to use military time, but then I haven't used it for many years now.

My wonderful wife recently gave me a Navy wristwatch with a twenty-four hour face so I now use military time again.

Military time is based on a twenty-four hour clock, with numbers on the face of the clock from one to twenty-four.

Most Navy clocks had two rows of numbers: the first row around the inside ring numbered from one through twelve, and the second row around the outside numbered from thirteen to twenty-four. Some clock manufacturers reversed the rings, but the clocks were the same.

The other thing rather difficult for me to learn was the ringing of the ship's bell. The bells tell you what watch it is as well as the time.

Bells don't coincide with the hour, but rather every thirty minutes the bell is rung. Beginning with one bell at 0030 (12:30am) and then every half hour thereafter, one additional bell would ring each half hour until eight bells, which would be 0400 hours, or four o'clock in the morning.

There would then be one bell again at 0430 and adding one bell every half hour until 0800 hours. This repeated throughout the twenty-four hour day.

One of the most important items issued to us with our equipment and clothes was a book called *The Blue Jacket's Manual.* This became our bible, so to speak. Blue Jackets are enlisted personnel below the rank of Chief.

The book contains information on how to do almost everything a sailor routinely needs to do. This includes knowledge such as a lot of naval history, terminology, naval customs, facts about ships, seamanship, and even pay and advancement. It is an interesting book you might enjoy.

The book also taught how and when to salute, and of course, our company commander made sure we had plenty of practice, but then, he gave us plenty of practice on most everything. Marching and calisthenics each required practice to perfection each day before morning chow call.

As I read my manual now, chuckles escape my lips every few pages, because of the old way of doing things and what I've seen change over the years. After all, the book is now over fifty years old.

Carolyn, my youngest daughter, bought the newest edition of *The Blue Jacket's Manual* for me. It is surprising the differences between the teachings and pictures of my original book and the new one.

She also gave me a new book, which I understand, is now being issued to recruits. *A Sailor's History of the U.S. Navy,* by Thomas J. Cutler, Lieutenant Commander, USN Retired, Naval Institute Press, who also happens to be the author of two of the newest versions of *The Blue Jacket's Manual.*

The book is quite interesting and became most difficult for me to put down. I recommend this book to anyone who is the least bit interested in the United States Navy.

It's not a history book per se, but rather stories about the Navy and Sailors. It wasn't written to glorify or name a few outstanding enlisted men or officers, like Admiral Chester Nimitz, as a lot of books do.

The book was written to tell the true story of the Navy. Included are a number of stories and details about blunders made by some officers and enlisted personnel as well as some of the defeats the Navy has endured.

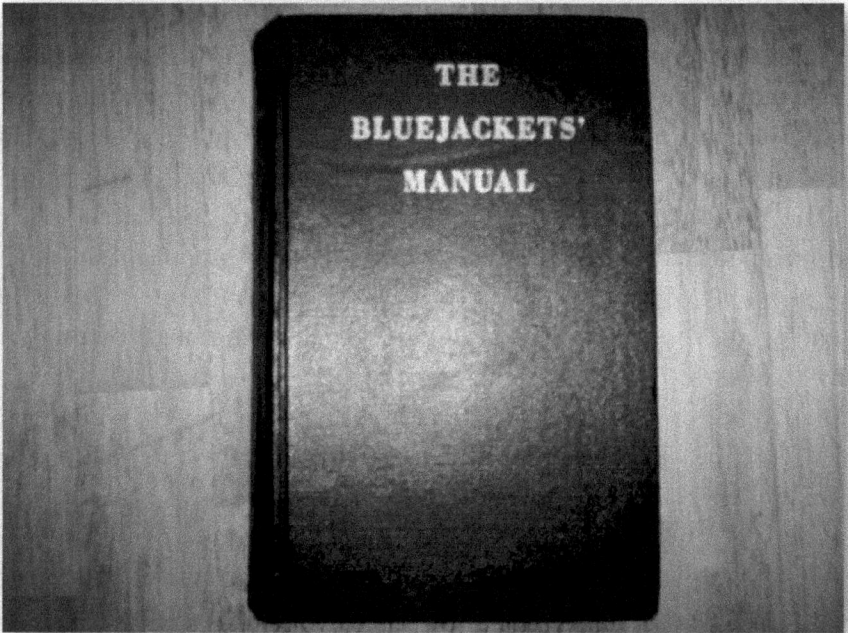

A Most Interesting and Informative Book

I don't know of anyone in our company who had any trouble going to sleep at night. Many of us learned to sleep while standing in formation when the opportunity presented itself.

The newness and excitement of life in boot camp soon wore off and most of us wanted, if not needed, more sleep than we were getting due to the long hours of each day. Lights out came at 2200 hours then reveille no later than 0600 hours and many days at 0430 hours the first three or four weeks.

I think it may have been more the physical aspect rather than the lack of sleep. We never stopped all day long.

Our time in boot camp was controlled and regulated down to the minute, including our so-called free time, with the exception of Sundays. Sunday, for the most part, we were allowed pretty much a day of rest, except we couldn't lie on our bunks after reveille.

We could do as we liked within the confines of the barracks and laundry area as long as our company commander didn't think of something he thought we needed to work on, which happened quite often.

On Sundays that we had free time to do as we pleased, many of the guys, including me on occasion, slept, everywhere, except on their bunks; on the floor, on benches and even on the long tables in the barracks.

We were given liberty call one Sunday after eight or ten weeks. Liberty is when one is allowed to leave the base and go to town for recreation.

The ability to go where and when you want is strictly regulated in the military, with total control in boot camp.

A few of the guys dressed in their dress whites and left for a while but I had no money so I stayed in our area and enjoyed my free time.

I'm amazed how after everything being so choreographed, the enjoyment one can get from just being able to sit backwards at a table or get up and go sit on the steps outside without asking permission to do so.

To be able to do things without being told you can't or you must do it this way or that. One begins to enjoy the simplest things in life.

One of the guys told me he intended to sell his blood when he got to town so he could get money to spend while on liberty. I still wasn't confident I could make my own decisions yet.

I had yet to get over my fear of being alone (although I wouldn't admit it then). I, like most of the fellows, stayed on the base and did laundry or studied and such.

When dismissed from our last class each day or from formation on the grinder if we were practicing marching, there was laundry to do. Everything we had worn that day needed to be washed, rinsed, and hung to dry on the clothesline.

The barracks had to be cleaned for inspection the following morning. Our brass and shoes must be polished.

If any time was left after our showers, we wrote letters home. The Company commander required us to write to our mothers at least once a week.

Seldom did anyone complain about lights out coming too early. Less and less often someone had to go to the head (bathroom) to finish polishing his shoes or brass.

The lights remained on all night in the head. Due to my lack of a sense of urgency and my tendency to procrastinate, I was one of those who learned the hard way to get things done before lights out.

As a result of having to do things in the dark and or not being able to go to bed earlier I learned to get the important things done first then play around.

I learned this lesson well and attempted to live by it all these years. I tried to impress upon my children as they grew up how much easier things would be if they followed this rule but not all of them learned.

The surprising thing for me, how tired I'd been every night. It was a different kind of tired. One with a sense of accomplishment. Even as an active young lad, I had never been as physically active in my life as in boot camp.

I learned over time, how to be more organized and do the hardest things first when possible, that way when you get tired, only the easier things are left to do.

The first few weeks of constant exercise turned out to be more than any of us, I believe, had ever dealt with before, but exercise couldn't have been any better for us. I think I gained at least ten pounds while in training.

My weight increased because of working harder and longer than ever before. I ate more every chow call which included eating a big breakfast every morning.

Mom and Dad always provided enough so we kids never went to bed hungry. However, I now know they sometimes did.

I didn't know we were poor. My brothers and sisters and me, didn't get everything we wanted but always got everything we needed.

The lifestyle of boot camp would be good for everyone. If you happened to be overweight, you would lose pounds. If underweight you would put weight on. If you were about the right weight for your size, you might lose a little excess fat and everyone gained muscle.

Boot camp turned out to be a good deal different from the lifestyle my parents provided as I grew up.

We received a lot of information in a very short time, and our Company Commander expected us to know all of it when he asked.

Much of what our CC taught was geared toward discipline, following orders, and to me, pride.

I took pride in my uniform, in my service and most important to me, I learned to take pride in myself.

It is difficult for me to understand why so many people don't take pride in their appearance or what they do. It seems to me, many people are not bathing and wear dirty, un-ironed clothes sometimes for days at a time.

These people don't seem to care how they look or what others think of them. Many people seem to be devoid of self-pride and it shows in their daily lives.

So many younger folks display poor work ethics, they don't respect others and many think someone else or the government should take care of them.

Some stand in line for hours waiting for something free instead of working those hours to buy many of the same things.

The Navy reinforced my father's teachings. If you want something, you must work for it. It may be hard to achieve your goal but, the sense of satisfaction when you do is in-describable. It might also be more important than what you wanted in the first place.

General Orders, were very hard for me to remember, at least in the proper order.

The eleven general orders are as follows:

1. *To take charge of this post and all government property in view.*
2. *To walk my post in a military manner, keeping always on the alert, and observing everything that takes place within sight or hearing.*
3. *To report all violations of orders I am instructed to enforce.*
4. *To repeat all calls from the post more distant from the guardhouse than my own.*
5. *To quit my post only when properly relieved.*
6. *To receive, obey, and pass on to the sentry who relieves me all orders from the commanding officer, field officer of the day, officer of the day, and officers and petty officers of the guard only.*
7. *To talk to no one except in the line of duty.*
8. *To give the alarm in case of fire or disorder.*
9. *To call the corporal of the guard in any case not covered by instructions.*
10. *To salute all officers, colors, and standards not cased.*
11. *To be especially watchful at night, and, during the time for challenging, to challenge all persons on or near my post, and to allow no one to pass without proper authority.*

I don't remember being asked about General Orders after graduating boot camp. I believe most sailors had them drilled into their heads and would remember at least some of them, even years later.

Standing watches, fire and security, turned out to be difficult for most of us in the beginning. We had never been required to get up in the middle of the night and guard anything, let alone a clothesline.

I remember wondering; who in the world would steal clothes from a clothesline on a Navy base.

Standing fire watches, weather on a land base or onboard ship, although very important, are boring and one might fall asleep if you didn't keep on your toes. Falling asleep on watch is a grave infraction and in time of war could be punishable by death.

Hygiene was stressed in a strong way. Living in close quarters aboard ship, no one wants to be aware of the person next to you smelling like an animal.

Even young guys like me who never shaved in their lives were told to shave daily anyway. A couple of guys who had quite heavy beard growth were told to shave again after lunch every day.

At least one person in our company, several times, caused us to be gigged during daily personnel inspection the first week or two for having dirty dirt (clean dirt is on the ground, dirty dirt is on a person). It was apparent they didn't shower every day.

I heard scuttlebutt about giving someone a GI shower (other guys scrubbing someone with scrub brushes). I don't know but some of the guys may have given him one.

However, after the third time of being gigged, we never got in trouble because of dirty dirt again.

I got into a fight one evening with a guy; the reason escapes me now as does his name but there is a good chance the fight happened because of my wise-ass mouth. He busted my lip hence the split lip photo at the beginning.

Only one punch was thrown, the one which split my lip, because just as the fight started our Company Commander walked into the barracks. Both the other guy and I popped to (come to attention). In his loud, angry voice, he asked what happened.

Neither of us spoke, and that made the Company Commander even angrier and he bellowed someone better answer him. I told him I walked into the door as it opened, which busted my lip (blood dripped down the front of my white tee shirt as I spoke).

He, for some reason, didn't believe me and tried to get one of us to tell him we had been fighting. It was just dumb luck we were standing in the foyer just inside the outer doors.

The other guy said nothing, and I stuck to my story about walking into the door, and the CC dropped the issue. The other guy and I got along fine after that.

⸙

I got homesick a few times, seeing planes in the bright blue sky as we stood in formation out on the grinder, and would wish I could be on one going home to my family, but I got over it.

To this day, I still look at the sky with little puffy, white, clouds floating overhead: if I see a contrail or a plane high in the sky, I think about boot camp and even lament sometimes about the good old days.

I've even gotten my wife, Diane, to guess where a plane is going as I do when she sees one flying overhead as we relax outside in the summer.

I got caught smoking outside by the wash tables one evening. The order had already been given over the loud speaker the smoking lamp was out.

That is the Navy way of telling everyone when one could smoke and when it wasn't allowed.

One of the fire watches grabbed my white hat and took off running. Everything we had was stenciled with our name or service number, thereby identifying the owner.

I was more worried about getting my white hat back or if I would get into trouble for having it stolen.

I had no idea my smoking after the smoking lamp was out would be a major problem.

The next day I received orders to report to Battalion Headquarters. Once there, someone ordered me to smoke a whole pack of cigarettes; the kind with a picture of an animal walking across the desert on the pack.

I smoked all the cigarettes with my head under a bucket while sitting on the floor in the hallway of B.H.Q. Some guy laughed at me as he walked past and someone rapped on the bucket on my head and told me not to smoke after the smoking lamp was out.

It was a nasty sight at the end. Tears flowed freely down my cheeks and my nose was running and nasty and I coughed like crazy. I didn't quit smoking though.

If I had quit smoking back then, I could have saved a huge amount of money. Not to mention the savings on medical bills and more important than anything else, the loss of my good health. Maybe I wouldn't have had a heart attack a few years ago.

Everywhere we went we marched, and if for some reason you were alone, such as going to Battalion Headquarters when summoned, you were required to double time it (run).

Calisthenics, drills, and marching took place every morning and then classroom in the afternoon once we got to camp Elliott.

Classes covered everything from Navy tradition, gunnery, firefighting (an in-depth multi-day class), and small arms.

We attended many classes including seamanship, where we learned the differences between rope, which is larger than one inch and, line and cord which is smaller.

We also attended basic classes on communications, including Morse code and semaphore, as well as basic survival (which I would learn much more about a few years later). Most of the classes were interesting, some more than others.

Somewhere around the middle of boot camp came a week called service week. The week each company of recruits worked in the galley, at least that's where my company worked. Reveille came at 0300 hrs. We had to be at the galley and ready to work by 0400.

Sometimes I worked in the scullery and washed meal trays or scraped the leftover food off the trays into garbage cans as well as carrying the cans to the dumpster. A few days I worked on the food service line.

I think service week was just a way for all recruits to learn to take care of other sailors. It saved the Navy money by not having to pay so many full time galley workers; recruits were plentiful and cheaper.

Swimming was another class we attended and I along with several others formed the group called non-swimmers. The instructors didn't put much effort into teaching us how to swim but rather how to stay afloat in the event our ship sank.

We separated into two groups, swimmers and non-swimmers. We jumped off a high platform to simulate jumping off a ship and we were instructed to jump in a position of attention.

It was scary but I, along with many others, had to be pulled out of the water the first time we jumped in, spitting and sputtering. We then were ordered to jump in again.

The tower rose almost up to the roof, and the water looked to be about a hundred fifty feet deep. I knew I had seen my family for the last time and I would never be aboard a ship, let alone jump off of one.

I survived the ordeal and jumping in the pool hadn't been quite as bad as it seemed at the time.

I became apprehensive though because I had never been in water over my head before.

I never understood why during our first swimming class, recruits weren't allowed to wear swim trunks.

We didn't even know we were going swimming until we got to the pool. (It wasn't called swimming, the class is called water survival, which just happened to be in a swimming pool).

We all undressed and stowed our uniforms in lockers and then took a shower. Naked and upon entering the pool area, we had to bend over and spread our cheeks for *dingle berry* inspection.

I guess they just found another way of teaching us not to question orders, and to make sure we showered well. I'm unaware if anyone failed inspection.

The next swim class a few days later, we took our regulation swimming trunks and towels with us but I still never learned how to swim.

I don't remember any classes I dozed off in as I did in high school, although the first class after lunch was sometimes a challenge. The worst class was the gas chamber, and there wasn't any dozing in this class.

After completing the classroom portion we received gas masks, taught how to put them on, adjust them, and make sure no air could enter except through the air filter.

They were very similar to the *SCBA*'s (self-contained breathing apparatus) we learned to use in the firefighting class.

Firefighting became an interesting class. However, I've had so much firefighting training since boot camp, what I learned then and in later schooling seems to run together. Some of the training becomes difficult to remember when I learned what.

The instructors herded us like sheep into a room called the gas chamber. We knew because a big sign over the door read, **Gas Chamber.**

My first thought when I saw the sign, was of the poor souls who were forced into Nazi gas chambers.

After tear gas filled the room, the instructors made us take off our masks, pulling them off of those who were reluctant. Not until everyone had his mask off (except the instructors), did the instructors open the door and let us out.

You never saw so many crying, snotty boys in your life as we ran out coughing, spitting, crying, and snotting all over. (This was much worse than when I smoked a pack of cigarettes with my head under a bucket).

One of the most interesting classes wasn't in a classroom, but on board the *U.S.S. Recruit TDE 1.* The *U.S.S. Never Sail,* is what we affectionately called her.

She didn't quite look like a building nor was she quite a ship. She became a two-thirds mock-up of a ship set in concrete. At the time she was a commissioned United States Ship even though she would never sail anywhere.

I don't know what anyone else thought the first time they went aboard her but when it became my turn I felt pride as never before.

I stood on the end of the gangway, saluted the O.O.D. (officer of the day), requested permission to come aboard and then saluted the ensign (the flag on the stern of the ship).

I had seen this played out many times on the T.V. shows *Navy Log*, and *Victory at Sea*, the programs I mentioned earlier.

This again, made me feel more like a sailor. Proud to be saluting the ensign and going aboard a ship. Even if only a scale model, I still had a proud feeling in my gut.

They taught us many things on board the *U.S.S. Never Sail*, coiling line, tying knots, much of which I don't remember anymore.

Mainly we practiced seamanship, drills and gunnery procedures.

We also practiced how to get from one part of the ship to another during general quarters. I must have banged my head enough times, I learned how to duck when going through a hatch.

The inventor/designer who thought of making a hatch (doorway) with shin and head bangers built in, surely got a good laugh.

Hatches on a ship are raised at the bottom and lowered at the top. This makes the opening smaller, which, in turn, makes it easier to keep water out.

When sailors wish to pass through, they must raise their leg to step over and duck their head at the same time.

Another thing is, when you close and dog a hatch, you should keep your fingers out of the way. I learned the hard way (the locking levers spaced around the hatch are called *dogs*).

Hatches are for damage control, and all hatches, whether in the deck, or overhead, or on a bulkhead, are dogged. All dogs are closed individually unless it is a quick-acting hatch which has a wheel which opens and closes all dogs at once.

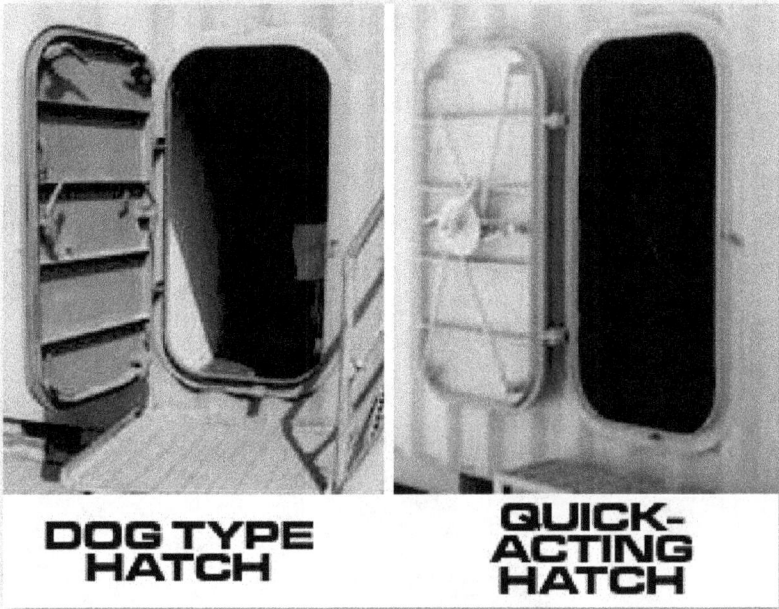

DOG TYPE HATCH   QUICK-ACTING HATCH

All closable openings aboard ship are marked with either an X (x-ray) a Y (yolk) or a Z (zebra) marking.

These indicate how secure the particular hatch is during various conditions which are set by the Captain. Openings with an X are the least water tight.

Condition X-ray is set while in port for normal working conditions except in time of war.

The captain calls for condition Yolk to be set when leaving port and while underway in fair weather and calm seas and no chance of being attack.

Condition Zebra is automatically set when General Quarters is sounded.

Zebra can also be set when the CO decides maximum security of the ship is needed as well.

I won't go into other markings found on hatches but suffice it to say the Captain can modify each of the conditions he sets and the other markings on hatches indicate which openings can be modified and for what purpose.

The front of a ship is the *bow*, and the back is the *stern*. When facing forward on a ship, the right side is the *starboard side*, and the left is the *port side*.

The floors are *decks*, and the walls are *bulkheads*. Stairs are *ladders*, and hallways are *passageways* or *companionways*.

U.S.S. Recruit (Never Sail)

There are no bathrooms; they're called *heads*, and rooms on a ship are called *compartments*.

A sailor doesn't go to work; he, *turns to*. Where applicable the same terms apply to Navy Aircraft also I later learned.

Muster is when a group or department gathers to make sure all hands are present. Lay-to is a Navy term meaning go to or come to a certain area, e.g. Duty officer lay-to the quarter deck.

Drills were frequent and varied. Every man aboard participated in every drill or emergency, as is done on real ships. He had a station to man and a job to do for each drill or emergency.

Drills promote teamwork, which is imperative aboard ship. My life could depend on what you do and yours on what I may do.

Some of the most important rules during drills and real emergencies are these:

1. Silence—only those in charge should speak.
2. Go to your station on the double using the following traffic routes: up and forward on the starboard side and down and aft on the port side.

These rules are important and eliminate confusion, congestion, and speed response times in event of an emergency such as a fire, which is the most deadly emergency aboard ship other than being attacked by an enemy.

❦

Many hours were enjoyed by all of us guys on the grinder (parade field), practicing marching and maneuvers: left turn, right turn, right and left oblique, and to the rear, which seemed to be the hardest for some to learn.

Our Company Commander wanted to make sure we had as much fun as we could stand I guess.

Inspections were performed every morning which resulted in many push-ups because someone had a button unbuttoned or had an Irish pennant flying (an Irish pennant is a thread left when the garment is made and has not been trimmed off).

If one person had something wrong, the whole company did push-ups. It didn't take long for all of us to realize we had to help each other get ready for inspections.

We marched everywhere we went, and we had to post road guards at every street we crossed. The second man, in the outer column on each side of the formation functioned as the road guards.

When given the command, "**Road guards post**." They would run out to the middle of the street, one on each side of where the company would cross, and would assume a position of port arms (rifle held diagonally across the chest), facing oncoming traffic and blocking it with his body.

When the entire company had cleared the opposite side of the street the command was given "**Road guards recover**," at which time the road guards would run back to their original positions in the company, join the formation and fall in step.

This occurred every time we crossed any street with vehicular traffic, regardless of time or weather.

I particularly liked learning the standing moves such as right and left face, but most of all, I became very good at about face.

This move started while standing at attention (all standing moves begin while at attention), and the order is given for "**About Face**."

When we heard the word "about," we put our right foot back with our toe touching the ground just past our left heel. When we heard the word "face," we turned our body to face the opposite direction on toe and heel then brought our heels together with our feet at a forty-five degree angle.

We didn't do the heel clicking thing like they do on drill teams. Neither did we slap our rifles. Our CC said he wanted silence (from us at least).

Each maneuver began with moving your foot, and each maneuver was supposed to be in unison with all others in your company. Some of the guys didn't know their right from their left, and the first few days of marching were total chaos.

Steps were supposed to be thirty inches, and people with shorter legs had to stretch out while guys with longer legs had to take smaller steps until everyone learned how to stay in step.

Without a doubt, the hardest move to make while marching was *"To the rear, March"*. Until everyone learned how to do it correctly the Keystone Cops weren't any funnier. The guys were falling all over each other. Some turning to the right, some to the left and some not turning at all.

I guess our Company Commander had seen so many idiots trying to learn some of the maneuvers, he had lost his sense of humor, because he sure didn't laugh at us.

Unlike the Marines and the Army, the Company Commander called the cadence and we repeated what he said. Cadence is designed to help keep everyone in step and determine the speed at which the company marched. It also helps relieve some of the boredom of marching; at least for me it did.

Some cadence calls are quite innovative and even funny. If you're interested cadence calls can be accessed online and there are many of them.

Remember, our Company commander screamed and yelled at us all the while, except when he was calling cadence, and he seemed to be able to see any mistake anyone made.

If you were fortunate, he would just yell at you, but if he was in a bad mood or pissed, he would make you do push-ups while the rest of the company marched around for a bit.

It took a few times for me to learn to keep my smart remarks to myself. Even under my breath, the Company commander either heard me commenting or maybe heard the guy next to me laughing. Each time I would be ordered to do push-ups.

It seems my mouth has always gotten me into trouble, but that will never change. It seems my mouth moves much quicker than my brain and I enjoy making jokes too much.

It's too easy for me to see something funny in almost every situation and I always wanted to share it with others. Try as hard as I might it seemed the Company Commander quite often called me; front and center.

When we were stationed together in Hawaii some years later he told me he couldn't keep from laughing at times at some of my wise cracks and jokes but he had to put on a straight face for the others.

Once, while in formation, our Company commander was instructing us on something or other, and one of the guys raised his hand. When acknowledged, he asked to go to the head. He was denied permission to break ranks. He soon peed in his pants.

None of us made fun of him at any time, but we learned to go to the head when we could, even if we didn't need to at the time.

One of the items of equipment we were issued was a WWI Springfield 30.06 bolt-action rifle which we called our piece.

Our piece was with us at all times except in the chow hall and in bed. If someone screwed up, maybe by calling it a rifle, then the Company Commander might make him sleep at attention with his piece.

We learned the sixteen count Manual of Arms, which are maneuvers of your piece in a specific way and to a cadence count. I don't remember how to do all of it now. There were sixteen different moves made with your piece.

There was also a twenty four and thirty two count manual of arms if I remember right.

Each hand placement a count, and each move of the piece a count. For example, moving the piece from one shoulder to the other would be something like four moves of the hands and piece.

Sixteen counts would move the piece from the ground to the right shoulder, to the left shoulder and back to the right with several moves in between ending with the butt plate on the ground again. I don't remember the moves anymore but I guess it was important at the time.

I think, after we had moved to Camp Decatur and had begun our nine weeks of recruit training that we went to the Camp Elliott Firing Range. We received M-1 Garand rifles for the day, and we learned how to load and fire them.

I had never shot a rifle before and that beast weighed a ton. I qualified as sharpshooter which I thought good for never having shot a gun before.

I remember being quite sore later, that son of a gun had a kick to it on my skinny shoulder, but it had been one of the most fun days of boot camp.

I loved shooting and the love of shooting and handling, even cleaning, any firearm gets my blood pumping even today.

A friend of mine once told me; "If you want to give me something give me a gun or ammunition or money so I can buy one or the other" and I'm pretty much the same way.

Guns are not toys but rather tools. I would rather carry one all my life and not need it than to need one and not have it.

Boot camp was pretty much routine after we moved to Camp Decatur. There were different classes each day, but we always started the day the same: reveille, your four S's (use your imagination), fall in, and march to the grinder.

By then daylight lifted its drowsy head, so we stood personnel inspection and then marched to the chow hall to eat.

Then we'd march back to the grinder, practice the many maneuvers our Company Commander wanted us to learn and do calisthenics, which made for a lot of fun on a full stomach.

We had noon chow, and then classes; the first class was the most difficult to stay awake in right after lunch, compounded by an instructor who droned on and on in a less than exciting class.

If we were lucky and had a little extra time after classes were over, our most concerned Company Commander, would allow us to repeat something he felt we needed to practice on the grinder. We then marched to the chow hall again but never ever before 16:30 hours.

I think the last week of boot camp we spent almost the entire week on the grinder practicing for graduation. I remember most vividly the part called the *Five and Dive*.

It was a five-count maneuver, and the important part was bending over with your piece propped securely against your legs.

Both hands went to your white hat and screwed it down on your head so it wouldn't fall off during the rest of the ceremony.

It took a little practice to learn just how to place your rifle against your leg so it wouldn't fall over and hit the ground which happened to almost all of us at first.

Anyone who has never been through boot camp can't appreciate all the noise a rifle makes when it is dropped and hits the pavement.

Every maneuver on the parade grounds had a cadence with music in the background, John Phillip Sousa, if I'm not mistaken.

When I did the different maneuvers and heard the music, I felt inspired to do the best I could. Perhaps it was designed that way, and if so, it worked for me. I was proud to be marching and strutting my stuff.

This may sound a bit corny to some but remember I was a kid, only seventeen years old and proud to be in the Navy. I was proud of myself for doing something I thought important and on my own for the first time in my life.

I had a twinge of disappointment my parents could not come to graduation but I understood the cost involved.

After graduation we recruits received leave papers and our orders to our next duty stations. We didn't get a paycheck while in boot camp. We didn't need money, all of our needs were taken care of by the Navy.

When we got our orders after graduation, we got a check for what was left of the pittance we were paid plus our travel pay to our next duty station.

I made more than I had ever made before, so it seemed like a lot (I think I made seventy-five cents an hour working at Standard grocery before I joined the Navy).

In the civilian world, Navy pay didn't go very far.

Travel pay is based on mileage in a straight line, from where you are to where you are going, as the crow flies, not as the roads go.

I believe my basic pay while in boot camp, as an E-1 was seventy-eight dollars a month, and when I graduated and became an E-2, the pay went to eighty-five dollars a month.

I had no bills, rent or food costs, so my pay every two weeks was just for me and I wasn't sure if I could spend it all each payday.

I had never learned to budget or even the value of a dollar. Before long I was out of spending money then I had to wait until the next payday to go on liberty again.

I had never paid any attention to how my dad paid the bills every pay day and so I had no idea what it meant to budget.

My orders were to report, after a couple weeks leave, to NATTC Memphis to begin Aviation Machinist Mate School.

As I said earlier, I liked the look of our Company Commander's rating patch and wanted one like it. I was going to be an aircraft mechanic.

I loved helping my Dad work on our cars when they needed it. Now I would be working on airplane engines. Boy, did I ever get a swelled head.

❧

I went home on boot leave not only proud of myself but received so much respect, love, and attention I became overwhelmed. I did manage to graciously accept all the attention from those who loved me as well as from the girls I met while at home.

I was only seventeen and I never dreamed of girls wanting to meet me before.

I suppose my head may have swelled a little bit, but I knew the attention came because those close to me were proud of me and those whom I met were excited to meet someone in uniform and I was lucky enough to be the one in it.

Even though I liked the attention of the girls, I was still very shy. I feared I would be perceived as being forward, as Mom would call it, if I asked for a date or even an address of any of the girls.

When I went to Memphis I had no one but my family to write to.

Even today, someone in uniform draws attention from those around.

Maybe it's because I am a veteran, but I always look for those in uniform, men and women. I look at their uniforms: Are they crisp? Are their gig lines straight? Are their shoes or boots spit shined?

If I have the opportunity to speak with them, I always thank them for their service.

I understand why most service men and women feel pride in the uniform and loyalty to our country's flag.

I will never understand why civilian citizens of this great country do not seem to show the same patriotism about their country until something terrible happens.

I've seen the American public up in arms and bad mouthing military personnel, and America, over one conflict and then become loud patriots over another. It makes no sense to me. We are Americans, or most of us are, and we should stand together at all times.

Any problem with the leadership of the country is not the country's fault; it's the people's fault. Vote, vote, vote! If you didn't cast a ballot somewhere, then keep your mouth shut; you've got no right to complain.

It is also my belief, you are not a good, patriotic, American. It costs nothing to go to the polls and vote, but it may cost you dearly, if you don't. Voting is not just a right; it is a responsibility.

Do your duty as an American and Vote.

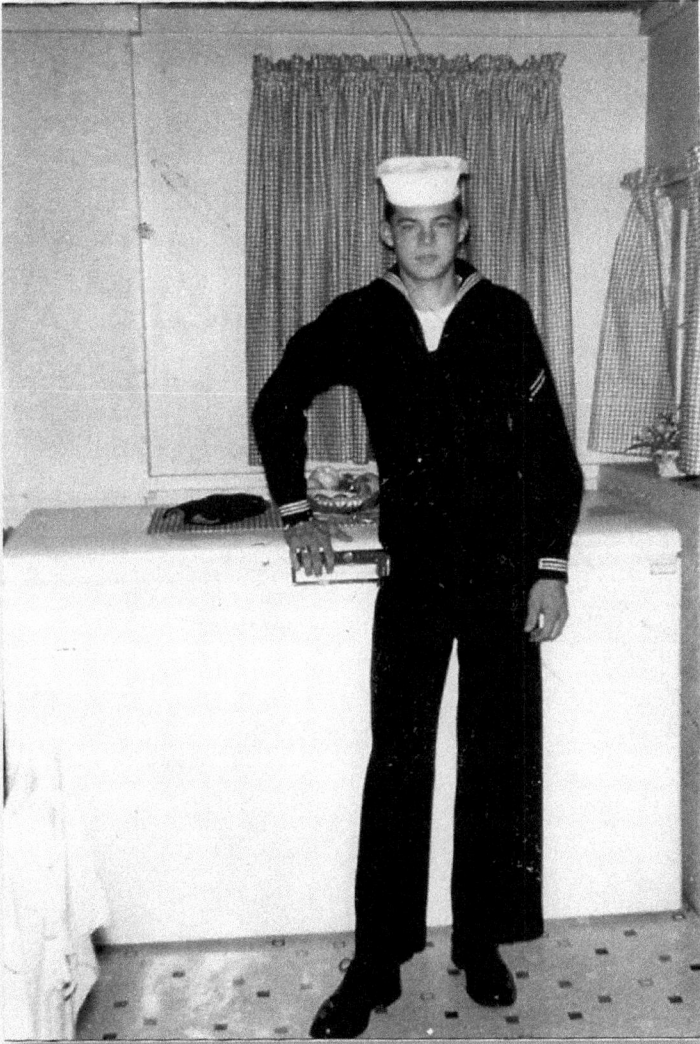

At home on leave after Boot Camp late 1962 before ADR school
What a scrawny kid!

CHAPTER 2

ADR School

After boot camp I received a promotion from E-1 to E-2, as all the graduates were and I felt proud to be in the service and proud of wearing the uniform.

The orders given me sent me to the N.A.T.C. (Naval Air Training Center) in Memphis, Tennessee, to attend Aircraft Mechanic School, after boot leave which lasted two weeks.

I wanted to be a mechanic on propeller driven aircraft. I didn't know the difference between regular engines and jets, but I liked planes with propellers.

At only seventeen I had never been away from home until boot camp. The Navy controlled every move recruits made, but when I got to mechanic school in Tennessee the only real structure occurred during school hours which meant freedom to do as I pleased for the most part after classes.

It took a couple of days for me to realize there wasn't anyone to tell me what I could or couldn't do, no Mom, no Dad, or Company Commander.

That's when it hit me, I am alone. I'm on my own and I got quite homesick. I didn't know how to take care of myself. I wanted to be on my own for a while and thought I had grown up.

Now I had mixed emotions, not wanting to be a kid but not knowing how to be grown up, and even worse I think, I wasn't willing, or maybe not smart enough to admit I wasn't an adult.

While in boot camp, I had little time to think about home, but now, I had free time in abundance.

At the time, I didn't realize I needed to be an adult; I thought I already was one, instead, looking back now, I still thought and acted like a kid.

I came to the conclusion I needed to do something to keep me from thinking about home. I went to the base library. I went to the enlisted men's club, but being under age, I couldn't drink.

However, they had Near Beer or three-two beer (3.2), and a couple of fellows told me I was allowed to drink that, and it tasted like regular beer.

My first thought; what would my Mom say? Would she allow me to drink a 3.2 beer?

I had sneaked a sip of my Dad's beer (Carlings Black Label) on a few occasions and knew what beer tasted like.

For the first time in my life, I made a conscious decision to do something I knew my Mom would not approve of; I ordered a 3.2 beer. How could she find out?

Looking back I realize the influence my Mother had on my young life and wish she could be here now to see how much I respected her.

There's not much alcohol in a 3.2 beer, and to get a buzz, one must drink a lot of them.

There isn't much chance of getting drunk because you get full fast and need to pee a lot, so I gave up trying.

Civvies (civilian clothes), were not allowed on base but I found out about a place off the base which rented lockers out and sailors could store their civvies in a rented locker.

Each time I left the base I went to my rental locker where I stored some clothes I bought. I changed clothes and caught a bus or walked into town; Memphis.

Once, as I walked to town, just after changing into civvies, I saw an officer in his car driving toward me and the base.

I hadn't been out of boot camp long and remembered the training our Company Commander had drilled into us about saluting officers.

Without hesitation, I popped to and gave the officer the smartest salute I could muster as he drove past me.

The officer returned my salute and I saw a big grin on his face as he did so. It took a few seconds after he passed by for me to figure out why he grinned at me.

I wasn't in uniform and it must've been obvious to the officer I was right out of boot camp.

I was overwhelmed with embarrassment and hoped no other sailors had seen the silly thing I did.

I went to town on weekends but had nowhere to go. I went to a movie theater a few times and to the USO on several occasions.

At the USO, I met a girl who volunteered there. I liked her a lot and I made a couple of dates with her. We met at the USO, went to the movies and maybe to dinner afterwards.

Only seventeen, I had no experience with girls. I felt the same as when at home on boot leave.

She may have been a few years older than me but it pleased me to have a girlfriend I could tell my buddies about but it wasn't anything serious.

I did make it home for a weekend a couple of times from Memphis. We had a radius of fifty or so miles from the base we could go on liberty in.

Indianapolis is a good bit further from the base than that but I didn't care because I met a guy in my class who lived in Indianapolis, and he drove right past my home.

He drove an old Studebaker Hawk I think. A sleek looking car, and driving at night, he went fast.

The first time I went home, I hadn't told my parents I was coming. When I got home, about three o'clock in the morning, I hadn't thought about how to get in the locked house and surprise everyone.

We left the base as soon as we got out of class at 1630 (4:30pm) on a Friday and planned to stay for the entire weekend, at least until Sunday evening when he would pick me up to go back to Memphis.

I hadn't a key to either door of the house I grew up in, so I started to climb through Mom and Dad's bedroom window which I knew didn't lock. WRONG MOVE!

Mom woke up, and in the dark, only saw someone crawling through the window; she grabbed a pair of scissors and came at me. I started yelling, "Mom, it's me!"

Mom screamed for my Dad to wake up, and I continued to yell, telling her it was me as I tried my best to back out of the little window.

I know I scared the beejeebees out of Mom, but she also scared me to death. I always called ahead from then on.

I found out the base had an Olympic-size swimming pool and swimming classes. I went to the start of a new class and found only little kids in the class. I wasn't going to sign up for a class with little kids and I had told no one I intended to go.

I played around in the shallow end for a while until I gathered the courage to try to swim and went to a little deeper water. I could stand up if I needed to but also swim if I figured out how.

I dove in and went a little ways across the width of the pool under water before coming up. I walked back to the side and tried again, and again and again. In time I dove in and made it almost all the way across the pool under water without standing up. After many attempts and much practice I taught myself to swim underwater.

Some guy, who must have seen what I was doing, told me I could do the same things I had been doing under water, while on top of the water. I learned how to swim, and from then on, I loved the water and spent many hours at the pool.

Although I didn't know it at this time, I would spend many hours in the ocean later on. I became proud of my accomplishment of holding my breath and swimming underwater. Soon I could swim the entire length of the Olympic sized pool underwater.

With more practice in the pool and later in the ocean, I could swim underwater for a little over two minutes which made me proud. Most people can't hold their breath that long even without the physical exertion of swimming added.

At least the swimming and school helped distract my thoughts of home and loneliness.

This aircraft mechanics school wasn't like being in high school; it was interesting, and I wanted to learn.

We worked on radial engines, something I had never seen before. They were nothing like a car engine in shape, but they used the same piston and internal combustion theory.

I had helped my Dad rebuild the engine in his car from top to bottom, a nineteen fifty three Packard Clipper. Dad and I stripped the engine down to the bare block and rebuilt it. We learned as we went and it took a while but the job got done and when finished she purred like a kitten.

I was fascinated by how the *radial* engines looked and intrigued by how they worked. Radial means the pistons are in a circle rather than in line like a car engine.

One thing I learned, which has always stood out in my mind, is the safety required for aircraft engines.

Unlike a car or truck engine where critical bolts are tightened then torqued. On an aircraft engine many of the bolts or nuts had to be safety wired together so they could not loosen up in flight.

It is rather an art to safety wiring in the proper manner, and necessary so the pilots, crew, and passengers would be safe from parts vibrating loose during flight. They couldn't pull over to the curb and stop if something went wrong.

After a couple weeks of classroom, we began working in an engine shop.

I had never seen engines like these before, and it fascinated me to learn how they worked. For those of you who have worked on car or truck engines before, *Radial* engines work on the same principals but are much more complicated.

After working in the engine shop for several weeks, the class got to go out to the flight line and work on real planes.

I will never forget the plane I was assigned to; a Douglas AD-2 *Skyraider,* number five. Her size surprised me; larger than I ever expected but I had never been close to a plane before, except flying to boot camp, and I wasn't as concerned with the plane as with the flight and why I was on it.

The early model *Skyraiders* are single seat, tail draggers. Classified as an attack bomber, with a four bladed propeller and a Wright R-3350 radial engine, which is the largest radial engine I ever worked on while in the Navy.

We trained on how to start and check out the engines while running them up to thirty inches of manifold pressure (a means of gaging how hard the engine is working).

This is the job of a plane captain, so we trained in areas of assignment that might be possible in the future.

Sitting in the pilot's seat and feeling that big engine come alive, was the most exhilarating thing ever in my life. I can find no words to describe how it felt to be strapped inside the cockpit of the aircraft, to feel the power of the beautiful plane under my control. I still envy every pilot who has ever been allowed to fly this plane.

I could not believe the power, the force exerted by this plane as I ran her up to full military power. I do not believe anyone who has never been in a pilot's seat of any aircraft can know the thrill, excitement, the heart pounding I felt.

I would learn other thrilling things as I got older, but this was the best I knew of at the time. It still ranks as one of the greatest feelings in my life along with taking the stick and learning how to fly later on.

I think only an aircraft pilot could appreciate how excited I was (and still feel now). It far exceeded the excitement I felt the first time I drove Dad's car alone.

The most common of the nicknames for this plane is the "SPAD" after the French World War I fighter. When used to help rescue downed pilots in Vietnam they called it "SANDY".

A beautiful plane
A-1H / VA-152 / USS Oriskany 1966

The Skyraider was manufactured by McDonnell Douglas, and went into service in mid-1945, too late for WWII. Not many were built until the Korean conflict and from then on a number of variations and improvements were made to the nearly three hundred manufactured.

Some of the later models were designed with two seats in the cockpit instead of one. One important point I want to stress is this; the AD could carry armament of 25,000 pounds, more than double the plane's own weight. No wonder it became, *"the workhorse of the Navy"*.

I learned firsthand while stationed aboard the USS Kitty Hawk how hard they worked this plane and how much the AD drivers loved them. One pilot even told me he felt safer in a Skyraider than in any other plane he had ever flown.

The Skyraider flew extensively during the Korean and Viet Nam wars in many different rolls from bombing and ground support to rescue helicopter escort.

I had the opportunity to speak with a Korean War veteran Skyraider pilot once and I envied him greatly when he spoke about a few of his experiences flying this plane I had such an affinity for.

Although Jet pilots in Vietnam looked down on Skyraider pilots in the beginning, many a jet jockey began to respect the Skyraider drivers for their ability to hang around and keep Charlie away until the Jolly Green Giants could rescue them after they had bailed out.

"Charlie", a shortened term for Victor, Charlie, (the phonetic alphabet). Used for North Vietnamese forces, VC-Viet Cong or guerilla fighters and NVA-North Vietnamese Army or regular army troops.

These terms are much the same as those used during World War Two, Krauts or Nazis for the Germans and Japs or Nips for the Japanese.

Wright R-3350 radial engine, 2,700 hp.
Note the many safety wired bolts on the engine

I think the school was thirteen weeks long, after six or eight weeks, a different instructor stopped in and spoke to our class one day. He told us if we wanted to test out of this class, the aircraft engine class, we would be allowed to transfer over to helicopter mechanic school.

I signed up, took the entrance exam, and tested out of the machinist mate school and passed both tests. I then began the helicopter school.

The helicopter school lasted only eight weeks so I would get out of school about the same time as I would had I not gone to helo school.

I found the class exciting and the engines I worked on were radial engines, like the ones I trained on thus far.

The fun and scary parts were the main and tail rotors. I was assigned to a *CH-19E Chickasaw* helicopter with a Pratt & Whitney *R-1340* engine. Quite a bit smaller than the *Skyraider's* engine, but didn't feel like it when you fired the engine up because you sat right on top of the engine.

You must realize, aircraft do not use mufflers like cars and trucks do. The exhaust from the engine of a CH-19 is below the cockpit on the port side. There is a lot of noise from the engine below the cockpit and from the transmission behind and above the pilots.

Without headphones or Mickey Mouse ears (noise silencing earmuffs) the noise from the engines could be deafening. I'm certain my Tinnitus, stems from being around so many aircraft engines turning up and not always wearing ear protection while in the Navy.

When the main rotor transmission engages, the rotor blades and tail rotor begin to turn, and that's when one begins to feel the vibration helicopters are known for. Some helicopters vibrate more than others do, as I will tell you about a little later.

With the rotor engaged and running the engine up, I could feel the power and the eagerness of the bird to go, to take off, with a slight raise of the collective. You could almost feel the disappointment in the plane when the engine backed down and she wasn't allowed to fly.

All the planes, students worked on and turned up, were tied down and chocked, but you could still feel the tug on the tie-downs, the readiness of the plane to take off. I'm sure not one student in class wouldn't have taken off if it had been permitted. All of us were excited by this part of the class.

One of the scariest things I ever did was to learn how to *"track the blades."* We learned how to see if the blades of the main rotor were all in line as they rotated. In order to find out, the engine had to be running, with the rotor engaged.

Prior to start up, the tip of each blade was marked with a different color wax marker so after the test you could tell which blade tracked where.

During the test, with the rotor whizzing around overhead, I used a long pole with a canvas strip, called a flag, attached vertically at the end of the pole. I brought the flag over to the rotor tips with great caution and let them touch the flag for a second.

You can imagine what might happen if the pole got too close to the blades as they rotated. I was scared to death but did the job.

After the test, you brought the flag down, and you could see by the colors left on the flag where the blades hit the canvas.

All of the blade marks should be right on top of each other; if not, one or more of the blades is out of track and needs to be adjusted.

We didn't experience any mishaps in our class, but the instructors told us how some students in the past hadn't listened and had let the flag go in too far, hitting the blades.

It seemed to me, similar to balancing a broom with one finger and making the broom go where you wanted it to go, a delicate maneuver.

Pilot and co-pilot both enter the cockpit from the outside, climbing up using the step attached to the bottom of the aircraft, then the toe and handholds above the step.

On the H-19, the pilot seat is on the right side and the co-pilot on the left. Different planes are designed so the pilot sits on the left side and some had the pilot on the right side.

Again, sitting in the cockpit and starting the engine of this helicopter was exciting. When I engaged the rotor transmission, the helicopter came alive. As the main rotor blades began to turn I could feel the aircraft begin to vibrate.

Each time I turned up a plane, helicopter or fixed wing, at any time while in the Navy my heart raced with excitement.

Our training, on the flight line, included everything a plane captain may be responsible for, making sure the helicopter was in tip top shape and ready to fly at all times. One had to go through the preflight list and make sure a safe plane was ready for the pilot when he arrived.

We checked the plane from top to bottom, making sure nothing was lose, from the main rotor down.

We checked to make sure all access panels were secure, oil and fuel full and a great many other things.

While on the ground, a plane belonged to the plane captain, but when a pilot got in the cockpit to fly, it became his plane. The plane captain made sure the plane was at its best so the pilot would bring her back to him when it would once again become his plane.

The H-19 flew a good deal during the Korean War. She could carry a dozen fully armed troops or eight injured troops on litters.

The plane wasn't fast but at around 100 miles an hour, the injured could get to medical aid much faster than on the ground, which saved many lives.

A few H-19's were used during the Viet Nam war but most were phased out when the Huey came along.

Rotor blades folded to save space

It is a two-man job to fold or unfold the rotor blades, requiring one man on top to secure or un-secure each blade from the rotor assembly, in turn so they will pivot and one man on the ground to use a cradle to lift and hold the blades.

The cradle is a long pole with a saddle for the blade to fit into so it will not fall or slide around while lowering or raising it. There is also a fixture, which mounts on the tail of the aircraft, to hold the blades in the folded position which is installed prior to folding the blades. All three blades are secured to the tail in the folded position.

The rotor system, the parts which rotate with the blades attached, is quite complicated. Both of the pilot's controls, the stick and the cyclic, are connected to the rotor by cables. No fly by wire here. There is no computer to control anything on this aircraft.

The cables control the servos and linkage of the rotor so the pitch of the blades can be changed and the rotor head itself can move in the direction the pilot wants. Everything is connected so the helicopter can move up or down and, with the help of the tail rotor, turn the helicopter in any direction.

Next, is a photo of the clam shell doors, inclosing the helicopter engine. At first I couldn't believe how flimsy these doors were. When they are opened the doors have little bracing and are made of light-weight aluminum. However when closed they are strong and withstand the vibration and flight of the helicopter.

Note the exhaust tube wrapping around the engine and no muffler as I said before. The engine is facing backwards because the drive shaft is attached to the rotor transmission which is above and behind the pilots.

If the same engine were attached to a fixed wing aircraft the engine would be turned around and you would see the propeller shaft instead of the carburetor which is on the back of the engine.

Engine mounted at an angle so the drive shaft angles
upward to the rotor transmission

Learning about helicopters and their operation, drive mechanisms, and different airframes, although complicated, was exciting and still is for me.

I didn't know then, but I would get to fly several different types of aircraft including helicopters in the years to come.

I would never become a pilot, but I did get quite a bit of stick time thanks to several pilots with whom I would fly.

I still regret never trying for my pilot's license even to this day. I realize it's never too late, so maybe someday.

Working on different engines turned out to be great, but the best part about school were the helicopters.

Working on and around helicopters and learning how to fold and unfold the rotor blades along with the many other things mechanics did was better than just working on the engines.

I hoped I would get orders somewhere I would be able to work on choppers.

We learned about autorotation, a method by which a helicopter can make an emergency landing, by watching a training film but didn't do it in school.

I would learn firsthand how autorotation felt a couple of years later though. <u>Very Scary!</u> I'll explain more on the subject a little later on.

In school, we never got to fly in any aircraft. All of our training was geared toward engines, props, and how the power is transferred to motion of the plane.

We also learned how the hoist worked and how to do inspections of the aircraft, making sure all the compartments and access panels were secure, and everything on the rotor head and tail rotor was as it should be.

I realized after getting to the fleet, my training at school had only been basics, and quite a bit more was to be learned. I continued to learn during all my time in the Navy.

I studied hard and listened to the shop chief. When the time came to take the test for E-3 I passed. The same held true when I studied for the *third class* or E-4 test although considerably more in depth.

It never occurred to me as a kid: I should, or could, continue my education and get my civilian aircraft mechanic's license, called an A and E license, for airframes and engines.

I learned I have always thought of myself as being much smarter than I am in reality, which caused me to miss several great opportunities.

I'm sure, if my intelligence had been as great as I thought it was, I could be an Admiral by now.

The free or low cost schooling available to military men and women is astoundingly abundant and yet few, compared to the total number of service personnel, take advantage of much of it.

I've met many men and women who had been in the Navy and the vast majority of those became officers after taking advantage of additional schooling as enlisted personnel.

I hope any young people who read this book, and will or are enlisted in any of the military services, will take advantage of all the benefits available to them and get the best education they can.

I know I'm still not as smart as I want others to think I am because I still think of reasons why I can't or shouldn't go back to school and get a college degree.

I'm getting older and can't do a lot of things I used to do but I know college would help me to write this and other books.

CHAPTER 3

Barber's Point

❧

I GRADUATED FROM *AVIATION MACHINIST Mate* and *Helicopter* schools, and was soon promoted from E-2 to E-3. Now a part of *naval air,* my stripes were green instead of black like an ordinary seaman, and I was proud of them.

Now I had become an AD striker. A striker is one who is working toward becoming a specific rating. In my case, I was working to become an ADR, an Aviation Machinist Mate Reciprocating (as opposed to an ADJ, Aviation Machinist Mate Jet).

When my orders to N.A.S. Barber's Point, Hawaii came, I remembered when my grandmother sent things to my sisters and I as children. She lived with my Uncle Jim when he was stationed in Hawaii while in the Army.

She sent little grass skirts and leis for the girls and I received a small glass jar filled with black sand from one of the beaches of the islands along with some other things but the black sand was the best.

I hadn't thought of that jar of sand for a long time and now I thought about finding a black sand beach. Although I searched many beaches on Oahu, I learned there were black sand beaches on the big island of Hawaii, so I never got to see an actual black sand beach because I never went to the big island.

❧

I was assigned to ship's company, as opposed to a squadron. I worked in the AMD (Aircraft Maintenance Division) the main hanger engine repair shop.

Although I wasn't aware at the time, I was given the nastiest jobs because I was new. One of the jobs given me was cleaning the engine mounting rings when an engine came in for overhaul.

Engine mounting rings are large circular steel rings with several mounting points for the engine and other mounting points for attachment to an aircraft.

The mounting rings had to be stripped of paint so they could be magnafluxed or x-rayed to see if they had any cracks from wear.

I used a paint stripper they called *monkey shit,* a brown foul smelling jelly like substance, which I brushed on, allowed to sit for a while and scraped off, removing all the green military primer off of the ring. I had fun but some of the other guys didn't like messing with the gook and cleaning up the mess.

I also worked in the prop shop for a time after I had been working in the engine shop for a while.

It was fun learning all the intricacies of different propellers. I was amazed at how delicate the balance had to be on them. Most had weighted shims placed in the hub of the prop for each blade but the fine balance was achieved by stuffing sometimes quite small amounts of lead wool in the hub also.

Trying to balance one of the big four bladed props could take several hours. The balance on any prop had to be dead on. The slightest imbalance could mean disaster in flight.

After working in the prop shop for some time, I learned so much about tools, in the engine shop and the prop shop, I was given the honor of being asked to start a tool crib for all the departments in the hanger.

I was rather good with tools and knew most of them on sight. I could look at a bolt or nut and knew what size wrench or socket would be needed or what special tool.

I was authorized to determining how many and what kind of tools to order, to stock the tool crib, based on how common each tool was, and how many might be needed at one time each day.

I had to devise a system so the guys working on the planes could check the needed tools out for the job they would be doing, and insure they would be returned to the tool crib which meant I designed and printed, new forms and came up with a system of record keeping as well.

Until then, each department had to keep their own tools on hand or go all the way over to supply on the other side of the base to get something they needed.

I received a small area in one corner of the hanger, about twelve foot by twelve foot, for the tool crib. I had a ten foot high chain link fence built around the area and chain link over the top to prevent anyone from climbing over the fence.

I got shelving and large bins for storage and arranged them inside after I knew what tools I would keep.

I organized everything in alphabetical order, keeping in mind Navy nomenclature, i.e. *Wrench, Combination, SAE 3/8*, I listed every tool on a *Tool Availability List* and every tool bin had a label with its contents.

Back then the United States Navy didn't use metric sizes on U.S. military aircraft much and so only SAE tools were needed in the crib.

There may have been other areas where Metric tools might be used but I didn't see the need in our hanger.

One other skill I was quite proud of having was my memory of phone numbers.

A good many guys, officers and enlisted alike, almost daily came to me and asked what the number was for such and such office or squadron or something and I could tell them immediately without looking it up in the base directory or going to the Honolulu phone book.

By the time I left Barbers point I had committed a few hundred phone numbers to memory. Most of them were Navy related but there were a few for the bars and night clubs I frequented on a regular basis.

Now, I consider myself lucky if I remember my own cell number without looking at my phone.

In the Navy, one needed a separate driver's license for each type or size vehicle to be driven. For a car or pick-up truck, a state issued license would do, and a Navy license would be issued.

If you wanted to drive a five-ton truck, you needed a separate Navy license. If it were a ten-ton truck, a separate Navy license would be required for that vehicle.

I was told to get a license for each because I might use either one to get supplies. In time, I decided to get as many licenses as possible.

Each class of license could be earned by completing at least a two-day school, and some licenses had a week long school. Each class had a test at the end to insure you had learned how to operate the subject vehicle.

Operate and drive had two different meanings in the Navy. Driving was controlling the vehicles movement but operating also meant refueling, checking all the various fluid levels and how to secure loads, if applicable and so on.

By the time I left Hawaii, I possessed many different licenses: five-ton truck, ten-ton truck, tug and Buddha licenses (used for towing and starting aircraft respectively).

I had three forklift licenses, the first up to six tons, a twenty-ton and a sixty-ton. I also got a tractor-trailer license using a box trailer; tanker trailers required a different license, for which I didn't apply.

When I found out one had to go to class for a couple of days for each of these different licenses I started signing up every couple of weeks. The classes acted like a short vacation from my regular duties.

The best part of having these licenses; I was the only one in the hanger to possess the big forklift licenses, and therefore I got the call to move some of the big stuff only the big forklifts could do.

Because I was the only one in the hanger who could drive the big boys I got a break from working in the shop on many occasions.

During my tour of duty in Hawaii several things occurred which I would like to relate. I don't remember in what order they happened so maybe I should have written this before I got old.

I took the G.E.D. test and passed, getting my high school equivalency diploma. This is a decision I've been glad I made for many years.

As I said earlier, I quit high school to join the Navy, something not allowed now, and luckily I had the intelligence to realize I had made a mistake in not finishing school.

I consider myself lucky because I didn't study, nor did I take any classes to prepare for the test. I scheduled the test through the personnel office, and three or four hours after I started the test, I finished.

I don't remember all my scores, but they were high enough to get my G.E.D. diploma.

I was proud of myself because I learned enough in two years of high school to pass the high school equivalency. Perhaps that was why high school classes were so boring for me.

I took the advancement test and passed, and promoted to E-4 or Aviation Machinist Mate third class (ADR-3). I was now a non-com (boy, did my head swell).

I remember my friend, Tom, told me someone had taken his jacket and was wearing it. I went over to Tom's area and found the kid working. He was an E-2 but I don't remember his name now. He was wearing a work jacket, and after checking, I found Tom's name stenciled inside. I put the kid on report for theft, and he went to Captain's Mast. I don't remember the outcome, but that was the only time I ever put anyone on report while a petty officer.

I learned how to manage those subordinate to me without resorting to harsh measures like putting them on report. I did it that one time for ego reasons. I know I did the right thing; just maybe not for the right reason.

This situation came back to my memory years later, when I was about to make my first arrest in civilian life. I made sure I was doing the right thing before I went through with it.

Photo of my patch

The rate and rating of the Navy indicates the pay grade, E-4, and the job description, *Aviation Machinist Mate*, respectively.

An Aircraft mechanic or ADR-3 as I was, the R indicates the type of engines worked on (reciprocating as opposed to J for jets); E-4 or Petty Officer third class is the lowest rank of Non-commissioned officer in the Navy. Equal to the rank of corporal in the Army and Marines.

When I got my crow, what we called the eagle on the patch, my Chief and a couple of other non-coms tacked it on. Tacking on was done by punching the new patch, which had been sewn onto the upper left sleeve. I was proud of my crow, and didn't mind at all the punches I received that day.

At another time, I also had the opportunity to fly (in the co-pilot's seat) a *HUK-1* (UH-43) helicopter, which I found to be one of the roughest riding helicopters imaginable.

The plane has twin main rotors that counter rotate at an angle to each other and look as if they would chop each other off, but they intermesh like a mixer or an eggbeater's blades.

Using the twin rotor configuration the helicopter needed no tail rotor. The engine is also at the rear of the aircraft which lessens the noise in the cockpit somewhat. The system works but causes a lot of vibration. I only took two hops in this plane because it rode so rough and I was not impressed. It also wasn't a good-looking helicopter to my way of thinking.

Because of the tilt of the rotors, one had to be careful and approach only from the front or your head might roll off your shoulders.

HUK-1 in flight

The two pilots I flew with, at different times, both loved the helicopter and said it was one of the hardest working choppers in the Navy.

I never got to know the plane as well as I did other planes, and maybe I should've, but at the time it wasn't my thing and truth be told, I didn't feel good about flying in it.

I've talked with others involved with the **HUK** who also think it's a great helicopter. A pilot once told me, "With enough power even a brick could fly". The HUK, I felt, fit into this category.

The Huskie was a rescue helicopter and carried two-rescue crewmen as well as the two pilots. It was a little faster than the H-19 at about 120 MPH. Because of these first few hops with pilots I had become friendly with that I began being invited to fly with more pilots.

I've found, over the years, no matter what kind of plane is being discussed, some will love it and think it's a great plane and others have their reasons for disliking it.

Helicopters now, are able to do so much more than those back when I was in the Navy, but those old planes did the job they were designed to do, and more, with less complicated equipment.

Another plane I flew in (again in the co-pilots seat) was a *Twin Beech RC-45J, (SNB-5P)* U.S. Navy designation. This was a twin engine, utility, fixed wing aircraft.

I flew with the same pilot, a lieutenant, a number of times to the island of Kauai, which is sometimes called the Garden Island because of its natural beauty. On several occasions, we would eat dinner in a restaurant at the small airport, before flying back to the base.

We flew whenever he needed flight time to keep his flight pay: a minimum of four hours a month.

I knew about the plane and its engines, but the pilot taught me a lot about flying the plane, and I got quite a bit of stick time.

This was the only fixed wing aircraft I ever had the opportunity to fly, so I don't have anything to compare to, but she was pretty easy to fly, after I got used to the controls.

I can't imagine a smoother flying plane or one more fun to fly. Thinking back now, I miss those flights.

Twin Beech RC-45J (SNB-5P)

Pictured above, the typical Beech Craft paint scheme, reddish orange on nose and tail and white, used for most of these planes bought by the Navy. This one has been restored with a lot of love and attention to detail and to picture perfect condition, as it was when in Navy service, by Mr. Taigh Ramey. WWW.twinbeech.com

Behind the pilot and co-pilot was either seating for passengers or sometimes-small package cargo. This plane, 585, was primarily used for aerial photography but there was limited seating.

Few frills but it gets the job done, in the tail section

This isn't the only extra seating though.

An Award Winning Aircraft

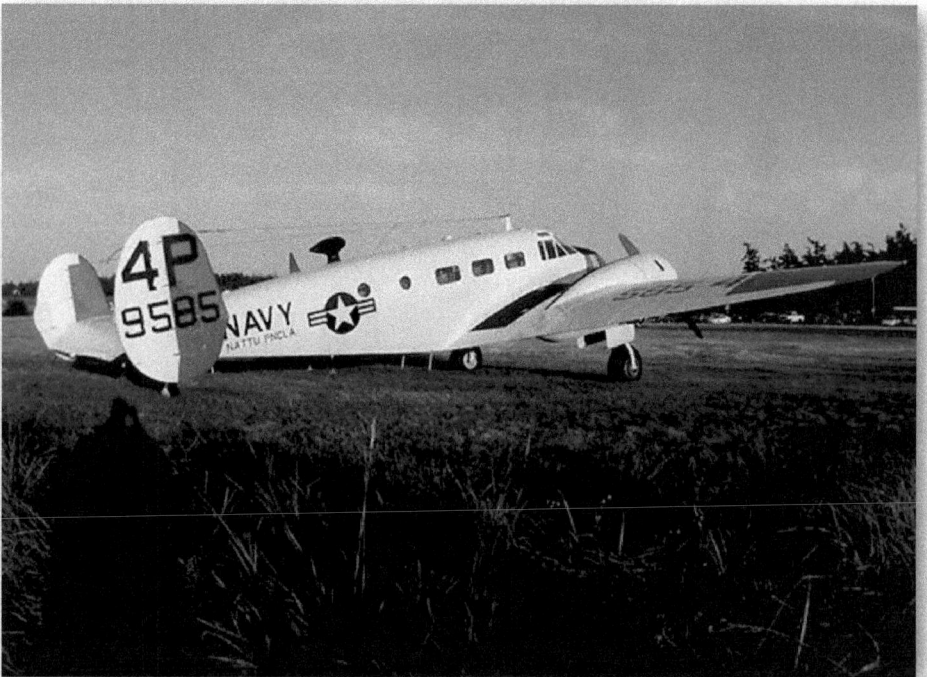

Another view of a beautiful aircraft

She is a beautiful aircraft and easy to work on. With two R-985 radial engines and I found them to be one of the easiest engines to work on, at least I enjoyed working on them.

The R-985 has a single bank of cylinders as opposed to two or more banks on bigger engines. The exhaust manifold is much simpler and the engine is easier to work on.

You can get to both sides of the cylinder heads, instead of having to find a way to slip your hand between jugs (another name for cylinder heads), to get to the backside of the one you're working on.

There is also much less to be safety wired. Safety wiring isn't difficult but is time consuming and it's important it be done right.

Using the yolk to fly the plane was a bit different for me because I had only flown in helicopters and they have a stick and collective.

The yolk is the white bar with the steering wheel. Pull the whole thing back and the plane goes up. Push forward and the plane goes down (civilian language). To turn, one uses both the wheel or stick depending on the plane being flown, and the rudder pedals. It takes a bit of learning to coordinate hands and feet, to turn smoothly instead of yawing the plane.

In a helicopter, you use the stick, or cyclic as it's called, to control forward, backward and side-to-side motion by tilting the rotor head.

The collective, which is at the pilots left side, regardless of which side the pilot sits on, controls the pitch of the blades, which makes the plane go up and down.

The pedals in a chopper also control the tail rotor pitch. Adding or subtracting pitch makes the tail of the helicopter turn left or right. Using all three control mechanisms the pilot can make the plane go where he wants to go.

The next plane I want to talk about has been a work horse for all the military services as well as many civilian businesses.

R4D is the Navy designation for the Douglas C-47. Another plane I have flown in but no stick time. The C-47 or DC-3, as the civilian model is called, has been around for a long time. The C-46 and the C-47 were two of the most versatile and hardworking planes used during WWII.

They flew supplies over the Himalayas (the hump) into China during the China, Burma, and India campaign during World War II (CBI). They also resupplied fighting troops all over Europe and many other theaters of operation.

They were also used to fly food and supplies into the American and British sectors of Berlin, after the Russians blockaded all ground routes to West Berlin, after World War II in Europe was over.

The plane has also been used in many other ways over the years. It has been and still is to some extent a popular aircraft for private owners because of its size and reliability.

R4D

Powered by two Pratt & Whitney R1830 engines

Their use during the Korean Conflict and the Viet Nam war was somewhat less, but they were, and still to this day, are a valuable asset in this country as well as many other countries where it's still a major passenger and cargo aircraft.

The Goony bird, as it was nicknamed, could carry upwards of 28 troops and their gear or 6,000 pounds of cargo. This plane has been used, in one variation or another since World War II and when I left the Navy in 1967, she was still being used.

I've read several articles about how popular this plane is with civilians even today and many military surplus planes and retired civilian airliners are being converted and customized for private use.

The *R4D* is a plane I enjoy looking at, flying in and working on. I see the lines of older aircraft as more artistic than those of today.

Aircraft design today is strictly functional with little or no thought of beauty in the design it seems to me.

The engines are a bit more complicated than the R985 but not as complicated as the *R3350*. Many times I became frustrated while working on the 3350's because there were some areas of the engines that couldn't be seen by the mechanic.

One had difficulty getting a hand into the area and only using his sense of feel to complete the job.

One other plane I was lucky enough to get to ride in one time was the Lockheed EC-121 Constellation. In the Navy, it was used for Airborne Early Warning as well as transport.

She had two radar domes, one on top and one under its belly. It was also one of the civilian luxury airliners of its time, without the radar domes.

She was roomie inside, with plenty of leg room due to the seat spacing, not cramped like todays passenger airliners.

The plane had four power plants by Wright. R-3350 eighteen cylinder, supercharged, radial engines putting out 3400 horsepower each. I had worked on a lot of 3350's so any of these engines could have been worked on by me.

Once while at Barber's Point, I was sent to the Marine airfield at Ewa Beach with a group of men to bring some Marine F-8 Crusaders to our base.

I don't know why the move but we did it. Each plane was wrapped in preservative paper, and the only way I could see was with the canopy up.

Each plane was towed by a tug and a man was in each cockpit to use the brakes of the plane when stopped.

We traveled the few short miles from MCAS Ewa Beach to NAS Barber's Point on regular roads and streets. We once had to wait for the power lines to be taken down so we could pass.

I had fun sitting in the cockpit and waving to the civilians standing along the streets as we passed by at a slow pace.

It must have been quite a spectacle for the families living along the route we took. It seemed like hundreds of people, including their kids, stood in their front yards, watching so many planes traveling through their neighborhoods.

I spent a good deal of time on a number of beaches when I wasn't working. Swimming, snorkeling and tanning. I remember once when I went home on leave my own mother hardly recognized me at the airport I was tanned so dark.

I spent hours in the water, as I mentioned in Chapter Two (ADR School) in Memphis. I learned to snorkel and dive for coral and fish. I learned how to make a Hawaiian sling, a spear gun type mechanism to shoot and catch fish.

I loved the ocean, and still do, I don't think there is any better smell than that of salt air from the ocean. It's so clean.

I also learned how to dive and harvest coral. Something I now know is not a good thing to do. It damages the reef, but at the time, most people didn't know this.

Someone taught me how to harvest and bleach the coral so it could be sold. Some pieces I brought up turned into beautiful decorations. After a while I realized the coral was far more beautiful underwater and still living.

To those of you who would condemn me: I'm reformed and feel deep sorrow for what I've done. As I told my Dad' many times for other reasons, "I promise I won't ever do it again".

Waikiki beach is for tourists and my friends and I stayed away. We went to a few restaurants and nightclubs in Honolulu from time to time but stayed away from the tourist traps except during co-ed season.

Then, many service men descended on Honolulu like a horde of locust to meet the girls on spring break.

My friend Tom and I rode our bikes all over the island of Oahu on the weekends. We camped on the beaches and explored any nook or cranny we found interesting.

For a time Tom and I were into rock climbing and cave exploring. We did real rock climbing not the wall climbing with hand and foot holds like in the malls now. We made our own grappling hooks and found places we could climb with the hook, line we bought, our hands and what equipment we scrounged on the base.

We had a blast, and as I think back now, it was a good thing for me because I didn't drink when we climbed or caved. It was something interesting and entertaining for me. I wasn't sitting in the barracks or at the enlisted men's club. I couldn't be on the beach all the time.

Once, Tom and I found a huge open cave, along the highway, high up in the side of a big hill.

We found a place to park his old car and walked back to where we could climb up to the opening.

We had our climbing gear and climbed up to the opening, which was almost big enough to drive a car inside.

It was obvious partiers had been there because of all the trash and beer cans thrown about. We also found a path others had used to reach the opening.

There was some graffiti spray painted on the walls but not a lot. I think it took Tom and me maybe an hour to explore the entire inside of the cave and as we were about to leave, Tom found a small opening at the base of the back wall.

We didn't have any flashlights and it was getting dark so we had to leave. We came back a few days later ready to do some more exploring.

We found, after digging loose sand out of the small opening, we could crawl through a tunnel through the rock. We had no idea how far the tunnel went or where it led to but it opened up into another large cave.

This room had no sign of anyone else having been in there, no graffiti or trash. Again, we explored every inch of this cave and found two more small openings, one of which was only a vertical crack in the wall and got smaller very quick. Neither I nor Tom could go far into the crack.

The other opening, this time a little larger than the first tunnel, opened up into a much smaller cave which we explored carefully but found no other openings. We later found out these were called lava tubes and caves. Remember, all of the Hawaiian Islands are or were formed by volcanos.

⬿⧉⧽

The small hole we found led to another room but much smaller than the first two as I said. It too had not been defiled. Tom found a few loose rocks, put them into a pile, wrote our names and the date on a piece of scrap paper and put it under the top rock.

Perhaps someday, Tom and I will have our names in world history books, as great explorers in Hawaii.

The crack, or perhaps fissure may be a better term, we only went a little way into, standing up and edging in sideways, before it became too narrow to navigate, maybe twenty or thirty feet deep.

My guess is the caves and little tunnels between them had been formed by lava from some long ago volcano and it didn't appear anyone else had ever been inside of them.

I also feel we weren't the smartest of spelunkers because we never told anyone else where we were going or when we would be back.

We were lucky I guess because a year or so after we had explored the large cave, the small tunnel we had barely been able to squeeze through before, had caved in. No sign of the opening existed anywhere.

I don't know if it was the entrance or the whole tunnel but one would need to dig a lot to find it and get back in. There was also a good deal more graffiti on the walls and lots of trash, which was a terrible shame.

⬿⧉⧽

One night we took Tom's car out to Makaha Beach and tried to find some girls who wanted to party. We found some fake buildings as we walked the beach and started to nose around.

We found a couple of small sailing ships made like old pirate ships only scaled down in size. We even found a building which contained movie film reels. We soon realized someone was following us.

We found out later the place was a movie set for the film, Diamond Head, with Charlton Heston. A security guard had called the police when he couldn't catch us.

We were fortunate in our decision to leave the set and go back to Tom's car when we did. The police stopped us as we drove past that portion of the beach a little later. We denied being on the set but one of the officers, a big Hawaiian man, told us if we came back there, he would put a bullet up our ass. We didn't go back until they finished with the set.

Tom's car was a reddish brown or maroon, older Oldsmobile or Buick, I don't remember which. It was a convertible which was great for cruising.

Once while at Makaha beach we found a surfboard with the front tip broken off.

The broken surfboard was useless for surfing but Tom put it nose down standing on the floor of the back seat and we left it for a long time. We thought it looked cool as we cruised around.

Tom and I both bought small, used, motorcycles. We rode them all over the island. We found old mountain roads and even foot paths we rode on. If we found a trail or dirt road, we had never been on before we would race to see where it went.

Several times, we were lucky to have slowed or stopped prior to riding off the side of a mountain on some sharp curve in the path.

One time the trail we followed ended at a gate to a field. We didn't see anything in the field and decided to ride in and check it out. We closed the gate behind us and leisurely rode the fence line to see where it went.

It hadn't been cultivated, and it didn't look like a pasture but a short time later Tom stopped in front of me, and I almost ran into him.

Ahead, standing under a tree, was a huge bull. He was maybe fifty feet away. We watched him as he eyed us a few minutes and we discussed if we should ease back or run.

The bull looked at us for a little bit and when we started to turn our bikes around, he made his move.

The bull charged and moved fast. Tom and I went in different directions but not intentionally. I rode as fast as I could in the field and found my way back to the gate Tom was opening.

The bull wasn't chasing us any longer but I went through the gate opening without stopping and I didn't look back to see if Tom was coming behind me.

I raced down the winding mountain side road without a care in the world, laughing inside over the silly bull incident, at least for a short time.

As was normally the case when we rode down a hill, I had switched off the ignition and put the bike in neutral and coasted. This saved a lot of gas which we didn't have a lot of money to buy. It also was a contributing factor in my accident.

As I picked up speed coasting down the road, the last time I looked at my speedometer I was doing a little over sixty miles an hour, I began to feel a vibration which turned into what I found out to be front wheel shimmy.

I switched the ignition on and tried to put the bike in gear but everything happened so fast I didn't even get into any gear before the bike went over.

The bike landed on its side on top of me breaking my left ankle in the process. My head hit the pavement so hard it tore my helmet off and I began sliding down the road with the bike pressing my leg down onto the road.

I began trying, then succeeding, to kick the bike off of me. I continued to slide down the road collecting an unbelievable amount of road rash over almost my entire left side until I came to a stop.

I tried to stand up and get out of the way of a truck coming up the road; but that proved to be most difficult. I was fortunate the truck stopped short of running over me for which I was grateful.

CHAPTER 4

Tripler Army Hospital

✧

WHILE STATIONED AT BARBER'S POINT I broke my ankle in a motorcycle accident and spent three months in Tripler Army Hospital. After only a few days, I swore I would never complain about Navy chow again.

I don't understand why the Army cooks are so different from Navy cooks. We had many of the same dishes like fried chicken or roast beef, stew, chili and other dishes. It seemed everything was cooked differently even the vegetables tasted different.

My broken ankle was a result of a motorcycle accident while racing down a mountain road I had been riding on.

I began having front wheel shimmy and I couldn't slow down fast enough. The bike flipped over on its side and I went sliding down the blacktop pavement.

I was wearing a helmet but the impact of hitting the road tore it off my head. I guess I was lucky to have been wearing one or I might not be here to tell the story.

The bike landed on my left ankle and broke it. I kicked the bike off me but continued to slide on the road until I came to a stop.

Thank goodness, there was an Army truck coming up the road. The driver told me he saw me sliding down the road. I slid right up close to the truck before stopping. I tried to stand up and realized my leg was broken.

I was bleeding badly from my left arm, from holding my head up off of the road as I slid, not to mention the road rash I soon found out I acquired.

The Army guys helped me into the back of their truck and took me to the entrance to their base where they called for an ambulance.

The soldiers tried to make me as comfortable as they could and they were extremely careful of my leg when they moved me.

I knew these guys were genuinely concerned about me and I hope they know I appreciated their kindness. I never found out who they were but I am most thankful for their kindness and concern.

It seemed like it took forever for the ambulance to get there and when it arrived I knew why. It was one of the old time field ambulances, I've seen in war movies. They loaded me in the ambulance and started down the mountain.

I asked why they used such an old ambulance. They told me they used a field ambulance because the new ambulances couldn't make it up the mountain. The new ambulance waited at the bottom to take me to the hospital.

Photo of similar Dodge ambulance below

Tom had been somewhere behind me the day of the accident, but said later he didn't see the accident, or see my bike on the side of the road, as he came down the mountain.

When he came to see me in the hospital, he said it had been a couple of days before anyone knew where I was. Tom went back up the mountain a few days later but never did find my bike or helmet.

By then I was over the initial pain of the accident and we laughed about being scared of the bull and how I flew through the gate and left him in my dust.

While in the hospital, after my motorcycle accident, President Kennedy was assassinated.

I became quite upset with the fellow who laughingly told me the President had been shot and I told him I didn't think that was anything to joke about.

I was in a wheel chair with a full-length cast on my left leg but if I had been able to get to him I would have walloped him good because he kept laughing about it.

Later I watched everything I could on television about President Kennedy. He was my Commander-in-Chief and some wacko shot him. I took it hard. I guess I had the President on a high pedestal.

To this day I still hold President Kennedy in as high regard as President Eisenhower, both of whom I feel were true leaders of the military, regardless of their personal lives: Ike for his leadership in WWII and Jack for the Cuban Missile crisis. Both of them were great men in my eyes.

The only other president I've thought had the best interest for the military and the country at heart was President Ronald Reagan.

After about eight weeks in the full-length cast my ankle was x-rayed again. The doctor wasn't happy with the healing and he put another cast on me.

I was lucky the new cast only went up to my knee and he put a rubber pad or walker on the bottom. Now I could get out of the wheel chair for good and not use crutches too much if I didn't need to.

Another eight weeks went by before the doc was happy with the way my ankle had healed.

During this time, I had been given duties to perform such as taking x-rays to doctor's offices in the hospital and delivering med supplies to different wards and other simple tasks.

The day after the short cast was put on.

At first I didn't like doing other peoples work but I realized staying busy made the time go by faster and I didn't have to sit and stare at the clock, I was able to do something and keep busy without rushing.

After the cast had been removed for good I went through another four to six weeks of physical therapy.

When I was released from the hospital, I transferred to the transit barracks at Pearl for a few days.

There I was given the option of requesting another duty station because I had been away from my base for so long.

I chose either the Boxer or the Bennington; I don't remember now, whichever one was in Pearl Harbor at the time.

Both were older ships, both had helicopters aboard, and I wanted to work on helicopters more than fixed wing aircraft.

I received my orders and personnel file and was about to get on the shuttle to go to the ship when my name was called to return to the personnel department.

When I arrived, a yeoman took my orders, gave me new orders and told me my C. O. (Commanding Officer) from Barbers Point requested me back. I had never met my C. O. and I never learned why he requested I be reassigned to my old duty station.

The only thing I could ever think of, was one of the pilots, whom I'd flown with several times, maybe had something to do with it, although none ever said anything during later flights together.

I returned to B.P.N.A.S. and right back to my original job, barracks and rack. Nothing changed. That seemed to please my best friend Tom though.

Tom and I spent a lot of time together. We worked in different departments but in the same hanger. Tom worked in a shop maintaining the tugs and Buddas.

Tom told me the name Budda came about because they were big and squared off, like the picture you may have seen of the big Budda in Japan.

Tom and I both made third class about the same time and because of his new rank, he was in charge of some of the fire or security watches in his department.

With Tom in charge, it gave him the opportunity to take a tug or Budda out for testing. Of course I took one also in case his quit working or something.

What we did was use the tugs to go off roading, something not yet invented for trucks, as they do now. Tugs are better suited for off road than Buddas. Buddas are wide and low to the ground. Tugs weren't fast but they had more ground clearance and they were tough and could go almost anywhere.

Not far from our hanger was a wilderness area almost like a jungle and that is where we went to "test" the tugs. We had a lot of fun for some time, until I turned twenty, which is the legal age to drink in Hawaii.

I don't know why I started drinking. Because I could I guess. I started having more fun, I thought, but now I don't remember.

I got into a competition with Tom and a couple of other guys to see if I could out drink them. I got drunk often but tried to be sober before time for the next muster. I never liked being late for work.

I've found over the years; many military men and women drink a lot. I don't think forgetting anything played any part but rather a lack of desire to do anything else.

Perhaps boredom was the reason. There have been many, many, things which occurred involving alcohol after I turned twenty.

I am not proud of them but none involved illegal activity except drunk driving and I am thankful that no one was ever hurt.

I was almost always a happy drunk and many times did dumb things to make those around me laugh. Making other people laugh has always made me feel good.

About fifty percent of the alcohol time I speak of was getting over hangovers.

Going to work in the hanger with loud noises all around, hammers banging, air guns roaring and people dropping things or shouting to be heard over the normal din, also planes being towed in and out of the hanger. The noise echoed throughout the big open hanger.

I can't remember how many times I've said, "never again", only to do it again a few days later. I guess I was a stupid kid after all.

Shortly after being released from the hospital I found out some of the guys in the hanger used the paint shop as a weight lifting room after working hours. They were glad for me to join them. A couple of the fellows helped me with a workout schedule.

It surprised me I couldn't lift the lightest set of weights the fellas had. Again I thought I was much stronger and tougher than I was.

They made a barbell for me to start with. Made from two big coffee cans, from the mess hall, filled with cement and a bar between them. The whole thing weighed right at fifty-five pounds.

At first, I was embarrassed about being so scrawny and weak but they didn't laugh at me and encouraged me to do the best I could. In time I got to the point I could use more weight and harder work out exercises. I began to put on some weight and started to see muscle definition.

I don't remember who they were but I thank them for helping me. One of the guys I admired a great deal, worked his butt off and was quite strong. I remember his biceps measured nineteen inches. He was average height but quite muscular.

I remember turning twenty years old and starting to drink. The legal age in Hawaii is twenty and I couldn't wait to start drinking like my boss in the engine shop. I don't remember his name but he was a First Class ADR and he drank a lot but he never came to work drunk or missed any work.

He lived off base with his wife and the two things I remember most about him were his sense of humor and his beer belly. I have no idea why I thought his beer belly was so great except that I liked and respected him and I guess I wanted to be like him.

It seems like I only went on liberty to go to bars and clubs to drink. I spent a good deal of time in the enlisted men's club, (white hat club) on the base when I was short of money to go to civilian bars.

I vaguely remember going to the beach with a couple of guys from my barracks, Tom was one of the guys.

He was my best friend and after I got out of the Navy, I went to see him in Niles Ohio once. I haven't seen him since and I wonder how he's doing. I haven't used his last name because I don't know if he would want to be identified.

We went to the beach one Friday night and I was drinking heavily. We met some girls and decided to go skinny-dipping. I remember taking my clothes off and running into the water but nothing else.

The next thing I remember someone waking me up and telling me I was going to be late for muster Monday morning if I didn't get up.

Tom later told me he and the other guy carried me back to the car and left me in the back seat still naked. Then they carried me into the barracks and dumped me in my rack when they went back to the base.

I guess I slept all weekend. I've had some hellish hangovers but this one had to be the worst.

As I've said before, I'm not proud of some of the things I did while drinking but I learned over the years many military men and women drink a lot.

I drink only on rare occasions now and only one drink at that. I learned, if I couldn't remember what I did, I wasn't aware if I had fun or not.

Near the end of my tour of duty in Hawaii, I went home on leave and came back to the base married.

She had been a friend in my high school but nothing too serious. While home on leave we hooked up and after a whirlwind courtship, tied the knot a week before I was due to go back to Hawaii.

A couple months went by after I returned to the base and she joined me after I rented a small house on the beach. The beach was just out the back door.

I loved the beach and the water and spent a lot of time swimming and snorkeling right out my back door.

The house was one-half of an old Quonset hut someone had bought from military surplus and converted into civilian housing. It was nice having a real home to go to after work instead of the barracks and my drinking slowed dramatically.

After a few more months, I got orders to NAS Ream Field, near Imperial Beach California.

The wife moved with me. I rented a small apartment in Imperial Beach California which was a short drive to the base. We lived there a number of months before I received new orders.

I was to join a group of Navy personnel as the helicopter crews on an ice breaker. I went on the cruise to Antarctica on the USS Glacier. My wife went back home to her parents and stayed there until I separated from the navy in 1967.

I'm getting ahead of myself now so let me finish my tour of duty at BPNAS Hawaii.

CHAPTER 5

Hard Lessons

❧

I FOUND OTHER CLASSES OR schools I might sign up for. A week or longer class was even better than being away from regular duty for two days for license classes.

I signed up for a survival and escape and evasion class. The first part of the class was about survival and the latter how to evade the enemy if behind enemy lines or escaping if captured.

As a kid, our family lived in a tent for several months when our rented house was sold by the owner without warning. I helped Mom and Dad with the chores, gathering wood to cook with. Making and breaking camp when we moved the camp site.

I didn't always do my job willingly or without complaining but I did what dad told me to do.

I hiked a lot and fished almost every day. I thought it would be fun in the survival part of the class and knew I'd have no trouble evading any enemy.

After all, I thought I was much smarter than an enemy soldier, I was in the United States Navy for heaven sakes.

It's been proven many times over throughout my life, my ego is much larger than my brain. I am aware of this, but I still keep trying to catch up with my view of myself.

The survival class imitated being stranded in a jungle, as if your plane had gone down, for example.

The only thing provided us, was some water to start. Later we needed to find and sterilize our own. We took turns carrying the water in five-gallon backpacks made of heavy plastic.

There were four groups of five or six men in our class, I think, and each group carried its own water pack.

Water weighs about seven pounds per gallon, so we carried an extra thirty-five pounds on our backs, as the group traipsed up and down the hills of the jungle.

Everyone took turns carrying the water but it seemed my turns came around rather quick. More often than I thought right but it was useless to complain.

We learned sand crabs on the beach are like popcorn and about the same size. They crunched like popcorn but had little taste. It takes a lot of them if you want to make a meal of them.

We also learned how to make gill nets for catching fish, which tasted much better than the sand crabs did. We picked what meat the little fish had off the bones.

We cooked them over an open fire on sticks and at first it was fun, until we started getting hungry.

We learned how to build a fire, tell which plants were edible and how to trap small animals.

We also practiced how to read a compass and find our way from a point on one mountain to another point on another mountain.

It turned out to be a lot of fun but also a lot of hard work, made harder when hungry and one hasn't found much to eat for a day or so. To deal with hunger is one of the hard lessons I learned about and, why it could be so important to learn survival techniques.

I didn't realize at the time, but the last day of survival training turned into the first day of escape and evasion training.

With a partner, we made our way from one checkpoint to another, then another and another.

We thought it was part of the exercises until the instructor at the second checkpoint told us about enemy troops in the area and we needed to avoid them.

If we got captured we would become prisoners of war. For me that became much more important a challenge.

The class became exciting and much more serious for me. I don't remember my partner's name but we made our way to each checkpoint, over the whole day, making sure the enemy had not captured the checkpoint first.

We quietly made our way to the bus we were to board. We watched the area for a long time and saw only fellow students milling around. We snuck up to the bus and found it safe from enemy troops and most of our classmates hadn't made it yet.

Without warning we heard yelling and gun shots outside the bus and several soldiers with red stars on their hats and shoulder boards stormed onto the bus.

Yelling in broken English they told us we were now prisoners of the *Red Republican Army.*

The rest of our classmates were herded aboard the bus with their hands tied behind them, they had been captured earlier.

We had to get on the floor so we couldn't see where we were going.

The bus drove for what seemed a long time and it was deathly dark when we stopped.

When we got off the bus, it was no longer fun and it took a lot of thinking to remember it was only a class.

The bus pulled into a driveway next to a latrine and a small building, where we all stripped and our clothes were searched, for what I'm not sure.

The guards told us to go into the exercise yard but to stay away from the electric fence and get dressed.

A fenced in area, with barbed wire all over, is where we were imprisoned.

Guard towers with machine guns looked just like the POW camps I saw in documentaries. It was rather scary to say the least.

Each one of us, in turn, faced long interrogation in separate rooms. We were required to tell them our name, rank, serial number and date of birth according to the Geneva Convention and nothing else.

The enemy soldiers tried their best to get me to tell them anything other than the basic information. They played good guy, bad guy.

One guard threatened to beat me, to take me out and shoot me or to shoot one of the other prisoners if I didn't talk. The other guard would ask to be left alone with me and tried to get me to relax and speak more freely but it didn't work.

They even showed me a coffin, a crudely built wooden box. They made me get in the coffin and they closed the lid and latched it. I thought that would be a good time to take a nap and I almost did fall asleep.

All of us were exhausted from the previous days of survival training with little sleep. One of the guards started beating on the coffin with his rifle butt so I couldn't sleep but at least I could lie down and rest.

They let me out of the coffin and put me back in the compound. In the center of which was a large cave like hole. I slipped into the hole and found a small tunnel at the backside. I realized someone had been digging a tunnel to go under the fence.

It was pitch black and I decided to get some shuteye. Because I was dead tired from the survival course and now the P.O.W. camp I just curled up as far back as possible and went to sleep.

I don't remember how long I slept, but one of the guards found me and dragged me out. He took me back into their headquarters and they started interrogating me again.

They roughed me up a little but they didn't hurt me; it was a class, not real life.

They made me angry during this interrogation, saying nasty things about my mother.

I didn't say anything because I didn't want to give them any ammunition to work on me with.

When they sent me back out to the compound I wanted to teach the interrogators a lesson for making me angry. I convinced one of the other prisoners in the class to help me escape.

It didn't take long to find out the fence wasn't electrified but if anyone got close to the fence one or more of the guards would start yelling and take the offender or offenders into headquarters.

When anyone returned from inside, the officers in the class asked a lot of questions about what happened and the floor plan. The officers in the class didn't act as if they knew what was best for everybody else. They just acted like officers when it came to making decisions but in a pleasant way.

I remember one officer asking me about my first experience inside the headquarters building and, I suppose, the decision to allow me to try my escape plan was approved by the officers.

I don't remember when, but at one point all officer POW's got herded into a corner of the compound and enlisted men were required to ask permission to speak to an officer.

My plan involved a latrine about a foot and a half high next to the fence on the right side where we came into the camp. A guard tower with a machine gun on top stood close by. We figured if I made it up on the guard tower, I would be able to jump down and be on the outside of the fence.

From between the latrine and the search building, only one of the guard towers was positioned to see anything happening at the latrine or the guard tower next to it.

If we distracted that guard, he wouldn't see our escape attempt at first.

Due to my youth, I had no doubt I could outsmart the camp guards and make the perfect escape.

I gave no thought what so ever to what I would do after I escaped. I had no idea where we were or the location of my base but it didn't matter at the time. Having just completed survival training, I was sure if I made it back into the jungle I would survive.

I wasn't aware of how much longer the class would be and I wasn't even sure how long we had been in the combined classes. Lack of sleep and food causes memory problems I guess.

One of the things the instructors taught us about as a POW was to cause the enemy problems; in any way possible.

My thinking; if I escaped it would make some of the guards search for me and leave fewer guards to guard the other POWs which might possibly give others a chance to escape.

It excited me thinking about the escape and I pictured myself as one of the movie characters on TV during their escape attempts. As the time of my escape attempt drew closer I began to become more anxious and wondered about many *what ifs*.

We decided if the guy helping me stood on the latrine, I could climb up and use his hands as a stirrup.

Lifting me high enough to get up on the guard tower wouldn't be a problem for him, I wasn't a big or heavy lad but my partner in crime was a rather stout fellow.

I wasn't sure what I would do about the guard sitting up there but I would see what happened.

After our plan got worked out, we talked to a couple of other guys and they agreed to cause a distraction on the other side of the compound. When they started the commotion, I would begin my escape attempt.

I saw one of my fellow prisoners had begun lowering the red star flag in the center of the compound. He and the other guy helping him started running around with the enemy flag and making a lot of noise at the opposite corner from where my escape attempt would be.

My cohort and I began to put our plan into action and I made it on top of the guard tower. The guard looked surprised as I appeared beside him; I guess because he had been concentrating on the flag guys on the other side of the compound. I kicked the barrel of the machine gun and the guard went flying out of his chair and fell off the guard tower.

I jumped down to the ground and took off running as fast as I could. It was dark and heading away from the lights of the compound I had no idea where I was going, or where I was for that matter, I just ran into the darkness.

I ran for a minute or so before two enemy soldiers knocked me down and pointed their guns at me and told me to get up. They took me back to the POW camp and again to an interrogation room.

I found out later there were guards stationed out in the fields surrounding the compound. At least I had created a little bit of chaos for the enemy.

It was odd this time in the interrogation room because none of the guards said anything to me. I was invited to sit on a chair and nothing more.

A few minutes later, a guard told me to follow him and he escorted me to another room, which bore a sign over the door, *Commandant*. When I entered some guy in an enemy general's uniform told me he was speaking as an instructor.

He let me sit on a padded chair and he offered me a cigarette and a glass of water. I took both eagerly. He assured me he was speaking as an instructor and wanted information about my escape attempt.

I didn't use any names or descriptions of those who helped me. He didn't seem to care about individuals but rather how and why we devised the plan.

We talked for a while and he told me no one had attempted an escape for a long time during the POW phase of the class.

He also told me not to worry about the guy who fell off the guard tower. He had been slightly hurt but they would do something to prevent them from falling off in the future.

He commended me for trying the escape and told me to tell the other people they had done a good job. I said nothing about the tunnel in the cave just in case he wasn't aware of it.

I went back out into the compound just as a couple of guards brought out large institutional size cans of corn, green beans and a couple of other things which I don't remember.

The guards poured the contents of the cans into a large metal garbage can, filled three quarters full with water, which had been sitting on an open fire for several hours. No one knew why the garbage can of water had been heating but we found out.

We also didn't know why a ten or twelve foot tall telephone pole stood in the compound, until after the class ended. It seems we were the first class to go through, that didn't suffer what was called, *The Apache Pole*.

We found out after the class, one of the POW students in the last class had a leg broken while on the *Apache Pole*.

The instructors used to make the POW's climb up, wrap their legs around the pole and had them tied. Guards would hit the student's hands with sticks or something until the POW fell backwards and hung upside down.

It seems they did this as a torture method to get prisoners to talk but because of the injury, they had been forbidden to use the *Apache Pole* that way again.

I knew from my experience during interrogation, the guards could be rather rough, but we all made it through without serious injuries.

After a short while, we lined up and got some soup out of the trash-can. We each got maybe a cup full in a metal bowl and a spoon and a few pieces of vegetable in the soup.

Most of us had little or nothing to eat for at least a day and a half. The soup was the best tasting thing I had ever eaten. There were no seconds and the little bit we got, served only to make all of us even more aware of our hunger.

It wasn't long before we realized daylight rapidly approached. I don't remember what day it was or the time but we were all glad when the Commandant came out and told us the class was almost over. A loud cheer went up.

We sat on the ground for a few minutes and listened to the Commandant / instructor speak. He told us we had completed the class with flying colors and our class had been one of the few to try an escape attempt and we should be proud of ourselves.

He also told us, capture by an enemy and becoming real prisoners of war, we should expect much worse treatment than we endured here.

He retold some of the incidents we'd been told in class, about some of the torture tactics other enemies had used in the past, similar to those used by the Japanese and the North Koreans. Extreme physical torture as well as psychological and emotional abuse, such as making derogatory remarks about one's mother, sisters or wives.

We got on the bus, which took us back to our base chow hall, where we ordered anything we wanted. I loaded up on bacon and eggs and toast and ate until I was ready to burst.

I went back to the barracks and took a long hot shower, which I hadn't done in over a week and it felt great. I went to bed exhausted.

I have always felt those classes, Survival and Escape and Evasion, were the best classes I've ever taken, bar none; including when I went to the police academy in later years.

I learned, among other things, I could take more than I ever dreamed. I endured more than I believed possible and the most important thing, never give up.

There is always hope and if the will is strong enough, anything, is possible. Failure to survive is not an option.

My dad has told me many times, "you can do anything you want to do, if you want it bad enough".

Sometimes one has to endure pain before he or she gets what they are working so hard to accomplish. It seems to me, the older I became, the smarter my Dad got. May he rest in peace!

CHAPTER 6
Ford Island

❦

AT ONE POINT IN TIME while stationed at Barber's Point Hawaii, I was sent, along with a few other guys from the hanger where I worked, to Ford Island in the middle of Pearl Harbor.

A few ADR's like me, some AE's, Aviation Electricians, airframe guys and a chief and an officer, made up the crew assigned to the temporary duty.

We were to change engines, with high hours on some planes going back to the states (engine changes are based on the number of hours running not miles flown). The planes were Marlin flying boats. I had never seen a sea plane before and looked forward to seeing them land in the water.

We arrived the day before the planes did and after getting everything ready, tools and such, we did a little sightseeing around Ford Island.

There's an Air Traffic Control Tower on the island and the same building contained offices and billeting which is where we stayed for the next few months.

The building was old, built before World War Two, and smelled old and musty from lack of use for many years but it became home for us for a while.

I remember when the first plane landed and was ready to be towed to the hanger. The plane crew attached the beaching gear and the plane taxied up the ramp and onto the tarmac.

I never tired of watching the planes land in the water and taxi around. Seeing the planes take off was exciting. Sometimes it seemed the planes took forever to get up out of the water.

If you are interested in seeing such dramatic scenes you could "just google it" (something my wife tells me all the time).

It took almost an hour for anyone to get the Budda started so we could hook to the plane and tow it to the hanger. The Budda was quite different from anything we used on the base at Barbers Point.

No key or any place for one and no one could find a start button. I'm pretty sure it was a World War II vintage piece of equipment.

By accident, when I was looking the tug over while someone went to find anyone who knew how to get the thing started, I pressed down on the base of the gas pedal and the engine started. The start button was hidden under the base of the gas pedal.

The Chief drove out to the plane on the flight line and we hooked the big plane up and towed it back to the hanger; I hadn't gotten my tug license yet and besides, no one ever tells a Chief he can't do something.

For those not familiar with the location of *Ford Island* it is where the battleships had been moored during the Japanese attack on *December 7, 1941*.

Many other ships were moored around the island and some had been sunk or damaged in the attack but the battleships received most of the attention.

The *Arizona Memorial* is on battleship row and we passed by when we left from or returned to Ford Island by ferry. The Memorial is much larger than the following photo depicts.

Arizona Memorial above its namesake

The super structure, the gun turrets and most of the other non-essential things like railings and deck fixtures have been removed. Part of the stern was blown away during the attack so it isn't visible in the photo like the bow of the ship.

The USS Arizona had been an impressive battleship before the attack and home to many sailors. After the attack the ship had been reduced to little more than scrap and a grave marker for most of her crew.

This is what she looked like before the Japanese attack.

It took a lot of men to operate this ship and a lot of them went down with her in Pearl Harbor.

Something that bothers me a good deal is, from the many things I've read about World War II and the war with Japan in particular, there seems to be little taught to the young Japanese in their school books about the war.

They don't seem to acknowledge starting the war with the United States by bombing Pearl Harbor or anything else for that matter unless it put the Japanese Army and or Navy in a good light.

I don't agree with the internment of Japanese Americans during the war. I do however have a problem with the Japanese government still not accepting responsibility for the war and what they did to POW's they captured.

It isn't about vengeful reparations, just accept responsibility

Photograph of Ford Island, during the Japanese attack on Dec. 7, 1941.

Battleship row is at the top of the photo where the plume of water is going up from an explosion.

Twenty-four years after the attack, when I was stationed in Hawaii, there was still much damage and evidence of the Jap attack on Ford Island.

There were even bullet marks on the buildings, hangers and the flight line where planes had been parked during the attack. A number of rusted hulks of small ships and boats sunk or beached during the attack rested on the backside of the island.

The one thing I've regretted for a long time is that I never took the time to visit the *Arizona Memorial*. The ferry we rode back and forth to or from the island went past the beautiful memorial.

The Arizona sat on the bottom plainly visible for all to see. The outline of the ship was clear under the surface of the water. I had also flown over the ship and memorial several times. I never took the time to go aboard the Memorial.

For about the next two months we worked on several (four I think) U.S. Navy, Martin PBM-5 Marlin flying boats. An adventure I won't forget.

The Marlin was gull winged to raise the engines and props higher above the water. She was powered by two Wright R-3350 radial engines with four bladed propellers. The engines produced 3,450 horsepower each.

The large plane had two pontoons, one on each wing, a crew of ten or eleven and the models we worked on had no landing gear.

In order for the plane to come up on dry land a crewmember, at times, had to get into the water with the floating wheels and attach them to the plane one on each side of the fuselage.

This task may take a good deal of time in rough water. A tail wheel was permanently attached to the plane so when the plane taxied up a ramp out of the water it became a tail dragger.

The detachable main gear looked like giant gas cans with wheels on them, red on the port side and green on the starboard side.

The plane couldn't land or take off from land with these wheels; they just weren't made to take the abuse and had no hydraulics or breaks.

The Marlin was a quite large aircraft as you can see the comparison with people in the photos that follow. Only one of these big planes would fit inside the old aircraft hangers at one time so the others sat outside on the tarmac to wait their turn for their engine changes.

The crews of the planes worked on each of their own planes while they waited their turn for the engine changes. They also received a good bit of liberty.

Some went sightseeing on the island of Oahu and some just went out drinking and partying. They all got more than ample time to rest and relax before we got their planes done and they left.

Each plane crew was a separate unit and the plane's pilot was the skipper or leader of the crew. Each pilot, as plane commander, decided how much work his crew would do and how much liberty they received. Most of them were pretty lenient under the circumstances.

The man standing under the bow hatch is Tom Bigley, CDR USNR-TAR (Retired) who piloted this plane some thirty-five years before this photo was taken.

Do you see the gas can with wheels that had to be attached to the aircraft after landing in the water? It's called beaching gear and the starboard or right side gear was green and the port gear was red.

The wheels had to be removed from the plane in the water before takeoff.

In areas where takeoff space was limited, the plane could be fitted with small rockets on each side of the fuselage called RATO. Rocket Assisted Take Off. Some used small jets called JATO or Jet Assisted Take Off.

It was exciting seeing the planes land and taxi to the ramp in the water and observing how the crew attached the beaching gear. Watching the planes labor to climb the ramp out of the water was almost painful. When on the tarmac they taxied to a waiting tug.

P5M-2 Marlin

Some of the last Marlins used by the Navy were Patrol Squadron VP 50 in 1966 for Operation Market Time. They were used for surveillance flights along the coast of Vietnam and retired from service in 1967.

This plane could carry a variety of torpedoes, mines, bombs or depth charges. The bulge on the plane's nose enclosed a radar unit.

If you peruse the last photo of the plane, you will see where the wing attaches to the fuselage. There is a small crawl space from inside the fuselage into the wing going to the back of the engine.

This location is where the oil cooler and the engine mounts are located. It is also, where I worked on each plane because I was still rather thin at that time and fit through the opening.

There is a hatch, which opens on the top of the plane, aft of the wings for access to the outer portion of the plane.

Along with a crane to lift, hold or lower the engines, a cherry picker, as we called the scissor lift, was also needed for the mechanics to be able to remove the cowling and work on the engines.

I don't know how much the chief knew about this plane but a lot of what we did seemed to be trial and error at first. Of course the crew and plane captain were around somewhere if we ran into a major problem.

By the time we finished working on the last plane we all knew how to do what needed to be done and did it just like pros.

I even got used to crawling in the hole and working with only a flashlight to change the oil coolers and the engine mounts.

Overall; it was a fun, learning, experience. My only regret is that I didn't get a chance to fly in one of these big planes. I would have loved to experience taking off and landing on the water.

Some of the crewmembers talked about how it felt to land on the water and depending on whom you talked to, the landings were sometimes rough and sometimes soft and easy.

As we changed the engines, taking one off and sending it back to the engine shop at the base, we would begin to remove the other engine and oil cooler.

By the time the second engine had been removed and prepared to ship back to the base a rebuilt engine would arrive for us to re-install.

When the first engine had been reinstalled a second engine would arrive after a complete rebuild.

When both engines had been replaced, they would be run up and test-ed. The plane would be moved back to the seaplane ramp, eased out into the water and the beaching gear removed when the plane became buoyant.

The plane, with its crew, took off and headed back to the states where I think the planes were to be mothballed.

It took a couple of weeks for each plane to be flight ready again and it was obvious some of the crewmembers were not in any hurry to have their plane completed.

I guess they knew when they got back to the states their flying home would be taken away from them.

When the job was finished and all the Marlins sported new engines and the last plane took off (all of our crew watched the takeoff) we packed all the tools and equipment up.

We got one more night of liberty and the next day we went back to the base and back to our normal routines.

I enjoyed the temporary duty on Ford Island. It wasn't always easy but it was fun working on the unfamiliar planes.

I was the only guy small enough to crawl into the tiny, black, space behind the engines to change the oil coolers and it had its advantages, like taking a nap from time to time when I wasn't needed.

Although all four planes were the same model and had the same engines each one bore its own characteristics. The interior was, for the most part, the same in all the planes but each crew had their own ar-rangement of some of the equipment.

Each engine was equipped the same, fuel and oil lines and electrical har-ness but with some differences in the line and wiring routings. Different me-chanics in the past installed some things in different manners and locations.

Taking things apart took a little more time due to the minor differ-ences in installations but the re-installment of the engines, oil coolers and other parts went a little faster and were all done in the exact same way on all eight engines.

CHAPTER 7

Ream Field

❧

THE TIME FOR ME TO be transferred came and I got orders to N.A.S. Ream Field at Imperial Beach California. I got an apartment for my wife and me in Imperial Beach.

It didn't take long for me to get to know one of the pilots and start getting flying time with him in a Bell 47. This chopper was quite different from others I'd flown in. I loved this plane because of the lack of obstruction of your view outside. Other than the vibration, it was like floating in air. I love to fly.

On my first flight in this chopper, I learned what it was like to *Auto Rotate*. The pilot asked me if I had ever auto rotated and I told him I hadn't and only learned about the procedure in helicopter school.

He told me he intended to practice today. Auto rotation is employed when the helicopter loses power. Without power you drop like a rock and, unlike fixed wing aircraft, you can't glide.

The rotor is still turning, driven by the air passing through the rotor. If there is enough altitude the pilot will push the cyclic forward to gain forward motion.

When the plane has dropped to about fifty feet above the deck (ground), the pilot will pull the cyclic back to raise the nose of the helicopter. This forces more air under the main rotor.

Simultaneously he pulls up on the collective, aggressively increasing the pitch of the blades to the maximum. This drastically reduces the speed of decent.

The plane may hit harder than in a normal landing but still with a margin of safety for the pilot and passengers and the plane as well.

To practice autorotation, the engine throttle is cut back, after the helicopter has started to drop, the collective is pulled up and slows or stops the fall well before getting close to the ground. The engine RPM is increased to flight speed again and the exercise is completed.

I only got to practice autorotation the one day and it had a pucker factor of about eight each time we performed the maneuver.

Shortly after arriving at Ream Field, I got assigned to a detachment, going on a cruise to the Antarctic, aboard an Ice Breaker. My wife packed up again and not only ship her things back home but also mine. She went home to her parents and stayed.

The ship, I learned a short time later, a US Navy icebreaker and in the process of being transferred to the U.S. Coastguard. USS Glacier AGB-4 would soon be *USCGC Glacier, WAGB4.*

Her keel was laid on August 3, 1953, launched on August 27, 1954 and commissioned on May 27, 1955. The ship was named for Glacier Bay Alaska.

The powers that be at the time decided not to rename the ship after being transferred to the Coast Guard so she remained the Glacier.

She was transferred and commissioned into the Coast Guard June 1966, after the Navy decided to give the Coast Guard total responsibility for icebreaker operations. This cruise I believe would be her eleventh *Operation Deep Freeze.* The Glacier was just over three hundred feet long, seventy four feet wide and a draft of about twenty nine feet.

It is my understanding this was her first cruise under Coast Guard control before being transferred from the Navy to the Coast Guard. Hence the mixed crew of eleven Navy personnel and two Navy helicopters.

The ships company were U.S. Coast Guardsmen under the command of Commander Franklin Faughman.

In fact, the Navy over time transferred all of their remaining icebreakers to the nation's oldest, continuous sea-going service, The United States Coast Guard, a proud service.

Since then, the Coast Guard has been the sole U.S. military service conducting polar icebreaking cruises.

We flew the two helicopters, from the base at Ream Field, one HU-13 and one UH-19 and landed on the ship. The Glacier, moored at Long Beach California, a couple days later set sail and left port.

We sailed towards Pearl Harbor, Hawaii, on the first leg of our deployment. I looked forward to seeing Tom again and having a couple of beers with him. The day came for us to shove off and begin our cruise.

An icebreaker has a round bottom, not "V" shaped like most ships and the reason is so the ship can ride up on the ice.

That is how the thick ice gets broken, sometimes up to twenty feet thick, from the weight of the ship, not plowing through.

I remember standing on the bow of the ship one evening, after being out to sea a few days, watching the sunset. This was the most beautiful sunset I've ever seen. We sailed south and west toward Hawaii. The water, almost glassy calm, with the reflection of the sun on the water was breath taking.

Many times I watched the water passing by the ship in the evening, wondering what the little green glowing things were. I found out later it wasn't phosphorous, as was widely believed back then, but rather light emitting organisms and plants or bioluminescence.

When I began to appreciate watching the sea, I began thinking. I realized I had become more than just a single Sailor; I was a part of the greatest Navy in the world. A part of something much bigger than myself, doing a job more important than anything I could have designed for myself.

I would discover things I didn't enjoy about the Navy; being apart from my family, the sometimes long, hard hours or the discomfort associated with a particular cruise, such as this one would turn out to be.

I was proud of the roll I played in the Navy. Proud of being a Sailor; proud of being a part of the heritage of those who had gone before me. I had in fact become Navy Proud.

USS Glacier starboard side aft looking forward

This previous photo shows the aft portion of the ship. Above the open part of the fantail is the flight deck and small hanger with two three-inch guns, one on either side of the hanger. These had been removed just prior to our cruise.

Looking a little more forward of that, if you look close, you can see the skipper's launch (the little boat high on the side below the stack).

There were eleven navy personnel in our detachment, three officers and eight enlisted men.

We took two helicopters, a UH 19 and a HU-13. As I mentioned before, the UH 19 was my favorite since I had been associated with it since helicopter school in Memphis.

It was a tight squeeze getting both helicopters inside the hanger but they fit.

At the forward end of the hanger, was a raised area the full width of the hanger and a couple of feet high made of heavy gage metal. I found out later this was the avgas (aviation gasoline) storage tank for our helicopters.

The next photo shows how the bow of the ship rises high and up on the ice trying to break it. Sometimes it takes several tries getting up on the ice before the ice breaks.

The Glacier could break Ice up to twenty feet thick. Sometimes the ice doesn't break and a ship will get stuck on top and another ship must pull it backwards to get the victim off of the Ice.

The Glacier had been designed and built with side, fore and aft heeling tanks to allow the ship to work its own way off if the ice didn't break.

Heeling tanks are like ballast tanks, used to change the stability of the ship, thus allowing the ship to rock or wobble itself off of the ice without help from another ship.

On our deployment, we pulled a couple of ships off the ice or broke a path through the ice so another ship could pass through. Then we found out why the skipper had a sign made on a previous cruise and placed facing aft above our hanger in large letters.

F O L L O W   M E

This became the ship's motto for the rest of the Glacier's commissioned life.

Riding up on the ice

This photo taken while still a navy ship, hence the GB4

The Glacier could make a top speed of about sixteen knots but most of the time stayed around twelve to fourteen knots or about 14 to 16 miles an hour (*1 knot (kt) = 1.15077945 miles per hour (mph)*).

She was capable of breaking ice up to twenty feet thick (As thick as two lanes of interstate highway is wide or as tall as an average house from the top of the roof to the ground).

It took us almost a week to reach Pearl Harbor and I'm sure one Ensign was glad to be off the ship by then. He had been seasick from the time we left port until we got to Pearl. This had been his and my first time aboard ship. I was a little queasy the first day at sea but I got used to it and wasn't bothered any further.

The Ensign went to the doctor when we got into port. After a couple of days he seemed okay again and sailed with us when we left port again.

The problem I found out the first week was an icebreaker has a round bottom, as I said before, but this causes the ship to roll more than conventional ships even in calm waters.

When we stood inspection on the flight deck, or standing still anywhere on the ship, you needed to keep your feet apart or learn to rock with the ship depending on which way you were facing.

This became kind of fun learning to walk and sway with the ship's substantial roll.

Someone told me the ships bell rang at eighteen degrees list and there must've been times it rang during heavy seas.

After we left Pearl Harbor, we sailed south and after a few days one of the ship's officers told everyone to prepare to cross the equator.

Anyone who had never crossed before had to go through the crossing ceremony, which included all eleven of us Navy personnel.

We were Slimy Pollywogs, and we needed to pay homage to King Neptune, Ruler of The Deep.

Not until after we had paid due respect and shown our worthiness, could we become Trusty Shellbacks, sons of Neptune.

Crewmembers who had previously crossed and recognized as Trusty Shellbacks, organized into *The Court of Neptune* to indoctrinate the Slimy Pollywogs, me for one, into *the mysteries of the deep.*

Physical hardships, in keeping with the spirit of the initiation, must be tolerated, and each Pollywog is expected to endure a standard initiation rite in order to become a Shellback.

Initiations are much less physical now and a bit more psychological. Even as late as the 1980"s, sailors going through the initiation rites have been injured and in the distant past even killed.

We didn't suffer any injuries or deaths on our cruise, but we were engorged with many humiliated sailors after the ceremony.

A lot of what happened to us or the things we were required to do was embarrassing but I had a good time and we all laughed at each other and in the end I think it was worth the hardship and embarrassment.

I don't remember for sure but I think we crossed somewhere in the vicinity of 0 degrees 5 minutes latitude and 164 degrees 8 minutes longitude, according to my certificate issued by The Imperium Neptuni Regis.

As we crossed the line, Pollywogs received subpoenas to appear before **King Neptune and his court**. These included his assistant Davy Jones and her Highness Amphitrite and other various dignitaries, who were all represented using the highest ranking seamen, who officiated at the ceremony.

During the ceremony, the Pollywogs undergo a number of increasingly embarrassing ordeals.

Wearing clothing inside out and backwards was required. Crawling on hands and knees, being swatted with swords made of wood or rolled newspapers and rather roughly forced down into whatever muck happened to be close by.

Some of us were locked in stocks and pelted with mushy fruit; some locked in a water coffin of salt-water and bright green sea dye (fluorescent sodium salt); crawling through chutes or large tubs of rotting garbage.

All this was disgusting, but kissing the Royal Baby's belly, coated with axle grease and ink turned out to be one of the worst things. The Royal Baby was one of the largest and hairiest, potbellied sailors I've ever seen.

When I, and the others I saw, went to kiss his belly, our heads were grabbed and our faces forced down into his matted, hair covered belly and smeared all over.

Hair chopping, seemed to be a lot of fun for the Shellbacks and was largely for the entertainment of the Shellbacks. Unfortunately for him, the ship's XO (executive officer or second in command of the ship) was still a Slimy Pollywog.

We all (the Pollywogs) received some shaving of our heads during the ritual but the XO wore a mustache for many years. The rumor was, he wouldn't let the sailor doing the shaving touch his moustache, until the skipper (CO) ordered him to stand still.

With his pants on backwards he let the Shellback shave half his mustache. I never saw him afterwards but one of our officers said he had seen the XO in the wardroom and indeed half his moustache had been shaved off.

So now I am a proud member of *The Ancient Order of Shellbacks* and proud to be among King Neptune's elite. I have my certificate and I'm proud to display it and I will never forget that day.

Before we went down on the Ice, we stopped off at the port of Lyttelton, New Zealand. We carried a load of *hands across the Sea* munitions for the New Zealand military.

For a couple of hours we all waited for liberty call while the crane unloaded stuff onto the dock. Because we were Navy personnel, aboard the Coast Guard ship, we had no duties other than taking care of the helicopters and our own gear. We stood no watches, fire or security, anywhere on the ship. When liberty call was announced, we went ashore.

We weren't on Cinderella liberty, liberty ending at midnight, like the shallow water sailors, (Coastguardsmen) so we weren't required to be back to the ship for a couple of days if memory serves me.

I'm not sure what I did those few days because I found a pub and began drinking. I did find I loved their dark beer. The tasty liquid was smooth and went down like water.

I remember sitting at a table talking with some locals. I never had any effects I've had while drinking my regular beer, until I stood up and found my legs had turned to rubber.

I remember going to Christchurch from Lyttelton by train. A narrow gage, electric train, (with two wires overhead just like the European trains or the trolleys of long ago), and from the inside, you would think it came right out of a western movie.

The inside of the passenger car looked like a cowboy movie train. Sporting wooden bench seats, two facing each other and then back-to-back, wooden floors and old time windows.

You could plainly hear the clackity-clack as the train rocked back and forth but sitting on those old wooden benches one felt every clackity and clack.

I think I enjoyed the train ride more than anything else in New Zealand. I don't know if the people liked us sailors or if they were just friendly people, but everyone I met treated me like a friend.

The Navy enlisted helicopter crew quarters were in the aft section of the ship and the officers had staterooms. I never understood why they called them state rooms.

Our officer's staterooms weren't much larger than a fair sized closet with two officers to a stateroom. The Coast Guard crew quarters were pretty much forward of ours.

I remember one of the evaporators, VAPS as they are called, went kaput on the way to New Zealand. The VAPS converted sea water into fresh water for use by the crew to drink, cook with, shower and cool machinery.

With only one VAP operating, fresh water for drinking became rationed and fresh water showers didn't exist. The fresh water produced could only be used for cooking and the ship.

Since there was no fresh water for showers, sea water was filtered and used for hygiene purposes, called salt water showers.

Salt water will get you just as clean as fresh water, although soap doesn't lather so well, but salt water leaves salt on you and when dried makes you want to go take a shower.

Anyone who has ever been swimming in any ocean knows when you dry off you are sticky and nasty and need to take a shower.

The salt water showers lasted for about a week and when both of the VAPS were back online everyone on board wanted to take a shower right away. It was almost comical seeing all the guys standing, with towels wrapped around them, in lines down all the companionways near a shower.

Over the bow with Icebergs ahead

Landing on flight deck

On flight deck

I soon felt clean and human again. The few guys who hadn't taken saltwater showers didn't smell any longer either. I don't think I ever appreciated how good a regular shower could feel until I took salt water showers.

One thing I had to get used to was working the hoist. The operator stood in the doorway and looked out and down to see the hook.

Of course, one wore safety straps attached to each side of the doorway but I often wondered how sturdy the strap and hardware were.

There was a difference in helicopter school; I was only a couple of feet off the ground while standing in the stationary, tied down plane.

In addition, it was sometimes hard to tell how far down the hook was when in flight. The pilot could also control the hoist if the crewmember went down on the hoist for some reason.

The rest of the cruise was rather uneventful. Freezing your butt off when you went out to launch or recover the helicopters and never getting warm when in the hanger or even below decks. Even while wearing cold weather gear, I still froze.

I guess that's why I hate cold weather, I could never seem to get warm and now, it doesn't need to be below zero for me to get excessively cold.

The older I get the worse it gets. Because of the cold, I did not enjoy this cruise much. I even spent extra hours working in the hanger because I didn't want to go outside to get to the passageway to go down to my bunk.

I felt like a zombie or something. I went out when forced to and worked or slept the rest of the time. I didn't pay much attention to what the other guys did except when we launched or recovered aircraft.

While down on the ice, the cruise became just an all-round bad trip. The ship shuddered each time she rode up on the ice and I wondered if the ice punched a hole in the hull.

I could hear the ship groan and the ice cracking. Sounds I never got accustomed to and never want to hear again.

The terrible screeching of the ice grinding against the hull was even worse when below decks and you couldn't see what the ship was doing.

The cruise became so bad for me; I wanted it to be over. I didn't care what happened or why. Where we were or going. When word came down we were heading back home, I just slept, if I wasn't working.

I'm not sure why I became so depressed, and the cold had to be the cause, but I was. I hoped I would never go on another cruise like this again.

This isn't something I enjoy telling about. I'm able to say I've been to the ant-arctic but have no desire to remember everything. I speak here only because it was, albeit excruciatingly unpleasant, a part of my Navy life.

The Glacier was de-commissioned on July 7, 1987 after serving some eleven years in the Navy and another twenty one years in the Coast Guard.

The Glacier wouldn't be considered a beautiful ship and with her round bottom she wasn't always fun or easy to work aboard. She was a strong, reliable ship and served her country and the men aboard her for many years.

I can't explain why it bothers me to know the USS Glacier is no longer an active ship or she may be cut into little pieces for scrap metal. She became my home for a time and she protected me.

CHAPTER 8
U.S.S. Kitty Hawk

AFTER OPENING THE WATERWAYS FOR the supply ships, to get into places like McMurdo station, we completed our deployment in Antarctica on the Glacier and returned to Long Beach then Ream Field.

I came due for rotation and requested sea duty; I never wanted to go on another cruise to Antarctica again. I received orders to the U.S.S. Kitty Hawk CV63.

U.S.S. Kitty Hawk CV63

Miss Kitty as she was sometimes affectionately called. A majestic looking ship I think.

The ship stretched a little over 1000 feet long, 282 feet wide at its widest, with a draft of 38 feet. She had a top speed of 33 knots (not quite 38 miles per hour) which isn't bad for oil fired boilers.

She carried a complement of about 5600 officers and men (In those days no women were assigned to ships). She was also the first and last ship ever built in her class, Kitty Hawk class.

The keel was laid on December 27, 1956 and she launched on May 21, 1960. Commissioned on April 21, 1961, a little more than a year before I joined the Navy and some four years before I would receive orders to board her.

When I joined the crew she was still like a new ship and looked the part. Her great appearance can only be attributed to the excellent maintenance by the crew.

Again I wasn't thinking ahead and didn't keep one of my patches. In fact I didn't save any of them. I didn't think about the memories I might have later.

I've seen some fine looking displays other veterans made for their memorabilia and wish now I saved more of my stuff. I've since found a couple of my old patches and I'm still digging for more of the things I should've kept.

Kitty Hawk won a Presidential Unit Citation for action off Vietnam during the Tet Offensive (after I served on her).

She also received the Navy Unit Meritorious ribbon award for exceptionally meritorious service from 26 November 1965-14 May 1966 (part of this time I was aboard her).

If I'm not mistaken our skipper was Rear Admiral James R. Reedy.

The USS Kitty Hawk took part in more combat missions in Vietnam than any other carrier.

I flew to Subic Bay, Philippine Islands, where the ship was undergoing preparations for combat operations off the coast of Vietnam.

I was assigned to Ships Company (as opposed to being in a squadron). I would be working in the repair shop located in the fantail below the flight deck.

My job included service and repair of Tugs, Buddas and other equipment other than aircraft. Working on small engines became a change for me but it wasn't bad duty.

Open blast doors looking into the repair shop

The blast doors remained open during fair weather except when recovering aircraft (planes landing). If an aircraft came in too low he would hit the stern of the ship and go into the shop then into the hanger deck (I don't believe the blast doors would be heavy enough to stop an aircraft from going through if it hit the doors).

I never got caught standing outside watching the planes come straight at me and pass a few feet overhead and land. I loved watching them, as they got ready to land. Still young and not bright yet, I didn't think about what might happen.

I loved standing on the fantail watching the sea, the turbulence created by the ship passing through the water, the screws churning and leaving a trail of white water behind us as far as the eye could see.

I had the same feelings while on the deck of the Glacier (before we hit cold weather). I was a Sailor and serving my country. I wasn't acutely aware of being in a combat zone but I became aware because of the daily activity on the ship.

Cat shots could be loud but nothing like the planes catching a wire. As the tail hook caught an arresting wire there was a God awful screech so loud you could hear it all over the ship including the repair shop below the flight deck.

The first time I heard the noise I didn't know what it was and it scared the hell out of me.

The ship design allowed for four elevators. One on the port side aft and two on the starboard side forward of the island and one aft of the island on the starboard side. I worked aft of the aft starboard elevator.

Replenishment didn't seem difficult during fair weather and calm seas but quite difficult during foul weather.

Two of the starboard elevators needed to be down in order to take on supplies on the hanger deck.

Quite often a swell would come over the side and into the hanger. Some of them strong enough to knock a man down if he wasn't careful.

As much equipment and planes as possible were taken off the hanger deck when underway ordinance replenishment occurred.

Most everything normally stored on the hanger deck in the path of ordinance movement was moved else ware on the hanger deck or taken to the flight deck and tied down.

Taking on normal stores wasn't so bad but during refueling or taking ordinance aboard, the smoking lamp was out throughout the ship.

Unless you needed to be on the hanger deck you weren't supposed to be there. We took on a lot of ordinance several times due to our mission in the Gulf of Tonkin.

Photo # USN 1097351   USS Kitty Hawk & USS Turner Joy refuel from USS Kawishiwi, 23 April 1964

Another shot showing the dangerously close ships while replenishing.

As noted above the photo, the oiler is refueling two ships simultaneously one on either side.

Not too long ago I had the pleasure of speaking to a man who had been stationed aboard an oiler. He suffered the misfortune of being knocked overboard by a careless crane operator while refueling two other ships.

He told me he had been in the water for over an hour and his ship was out of sight before being rescued by a tin can (Destroyer).

He said he prayed he would be picked up and scared he might be eaten by a shark.

❦

With a little practice, these ladders can be negotiated using no steps going down (you don't go down backwards). I learned how by placing my hands and forearms on the hand rails or chains, push my feet out in front of me slightly and slide down. Gravity would help one descend but not so fast as to cause a hard landing.

Looking up from the bottom of a ladder

The chains used as hand rails couldn't be any more polished or smooth if they had been polished by a machine. They wore smooth and shiny from hundreds of hands sliding down them on a daily basis.

Once after taking on bombs, for the planes to drop over Vietnam, a kid fell overboard.

The bombs came over on wooden pallets during a replenishment run with a supply ship. After storing the bombs, ordinance guys stacked the pallets on an elevator then threw them overboard.

Protocol said to push them over the side one at a time and scoot them on the deck as they did so.

One of the kids was skylarking, (a term used in the Navy to define playing around or activity not connected with the work at hand) and picking the pallets up over his head and throwing them overboard.

The wind caught one of them as he held the pallet up over his head and he went sailing off the elevator with the pallet. This according to a witness.

I was working in the shop when the alarm sounded, *Man Overboard*; several of us went to the fantail and saw the kid floating in the water holding onto the pallet. Luckily he wasn't sucked under the ship and spit out by the screws.

When the alarm sounded and other ships in the area were notified all kinds of sirens and bells started going off.

The Angel (rescue helicopter), took off from the flight deck and we saw the closest tin can, (destroyer) made a sharp turn and headed for the guy in the water.

I never saw a ship move so fast or make such violent turns as the destroyer did. The Angel got to the kid first, rescued him, and brought him back to the ship.

I found out later, one of the incentives for the tin can to try so hard to rescue the boy; if they had rescued him our ship would give them ice cream.

Ice cream we took for granted because we had some any time we wanted. A Destroyer couldn't store much so they didn't enjoy any for long periods.

I've talked to a couple of tin can sailors and they both confirmed the desire to rescue, 1. Anyone in need and 2. Someone overboard from a larger ship, like a carrier.

I only heard second hand what happened to the kid who fell over-board so I don't know for sure. Scuttlebutt said, the kid got a Captain's Mast and lost a stripe as well as brig time. I'm sure that wasn't too far off the mark.

The kid was in the water for a little less than fifteen minutes as I remem-ber but that fifteen minutes cost the Navy several thousands of dollars.

One good thing about the Kitty Hawk was the food. They had a large regular galley and they had a small diner like galley where you could get cooked to order burgers and such.

Even the regular galley food was like going to a restaurant, except you ate off of metal trays, but the food tasted good, much better than the food I ate while in Tripler Army hospital.

Officers also had their own galley and dining area, called a wardroom.

We sailed through the South China Sea and into the Gulf of Tonkin so our squadron planes could carry out their missions over Vietnam.

I don't know where our planes went or what they bombed but Hanoi and Haiphong were both within our planes range.

To my knowledge, we didn't lose any planes to enemy fire but I heard a couple had come back aboard with damage.

One thing that bothered me several times, might we, the Kitty Hawk and her crew, come under attack from the North Vietnamese Air Force or Navy as had happened in the past? I never said anything to anyone because I didn't want anybody to think I was scared.

My thinking; if our planes were able to fly out to land on the ship, why couldn't an enemy plane fly out to attack us?

I know we had good protection against an attack from the air but that may not stop the North Vietnamese from trying.

I only had passing thoughts about being attacked by a surface craft or even a submarine. I didn't think the enemy had anything which could attack an aircraft carrier other than planes anymore.

Never the less, I made sure I knew how to get to the closest gun emplacement. I knew I could operate a fifty caliber if I must.

I was concerned we might be attacked by air. After all, we were getting combat pay so there must've been some risk.

During my two tours in the Gulf of Tonkin in 1966-67, we lost no planes or pilots I am aware of. Losses occurred by the Kitty Hawk in June of 1964, March of 1967 and again in January 1968, most due to AAA.

Do you remember what plane I loved most at the beginning of this story? If you guessed the AD Skyraider, you are correct and when I saw them on the ship, I became ecstatic to say the least.

I learned Skyraiders worked continuously flying bombing and attack missions over Vietnam and I might get to see them fly.

I went to the flight deck any time I could if launching or recovering Skyraiders. I always felt the Skyraiders carried more armament attached to them than any other planes flying missions over North Vietnam.

Many times I longed to be able to go on a flight, in one of the two seaters, as I watched them take off or land.

Not long ago, I had the privilege of meeting one of the Skyraider drivers, who flew missions over Vietnam.

Although he had been land based I still enjoyed talking with him for the short time we spent together. He seemed quite pleased I had been familiar with the aircraft he loved to fly.

Sky Raiders became one of the most loved, hardworking and dependable planes of its day. They could absorb tremendous battle damage and still bring her pilot home, even if she was incapable of ever flying again.

The Sky Raider has always been such a great plane. Even as a propeller driven aircraft, there was an attempt a few years after the plane was gone from the military to bring her back with a few new modifications.

When Douglas Aircraft was asked about re-tooling and building more Sky Raiders, the cost was prohibitive and no more would be built.

A beautiful workhorse

Please note to the left of the star and bar and above NAVY is the ship to which the plane is attached.

In this case, my ship, USS Kitty Hawk.

I never got the opportunity to fly in a Skyraider because they only flew on specific missions off the ship but, if allowed, I would've gone in a heartbeat. Maybe someday I will have a chance to take a hop in one.

There are four arresting cables, wires as we call them, the third wire is the one the pilots try to catch. Catching the one or two wire doesn't get a good score for the landing and catching the number four wire is dangerous.

A pilot uses full power when he's landing on a carrier so if he *bolts,* or misses all four wires, he can lift off and go around again for another try.

Every landing is scored by the LSO's, *Landing Signal officers,* who are also carrier pilots. The landing is later discussed with each pilot. Even the most experienced pilots get scored and critiqued later in the ready room.

The landing scoring covers all aspects of each landing, angle, speed, pitch and several other things. All landings are videotaped and every pilot watches his landing during debriefing.

Even in good weather and in the daylight, landing on a moving carrier is no walk in the park.

Trying to land in the dark and on a pitching, rolling deck is the most difficult routine maneuver any pilot can accomplish. Some never get the hang of it and must be assigned to dry land bases somewhere.

Of the many pilots I've talked with, all without exception, respect and revere carrier pilots the most regardless of which branch of service.

Since women have become combat pilots and are being assigned to carriers, they also are much more respected than in years past.

I've talked with a few pilots after I got out of the Navy, including an F-4 Phantom driver who served in Nam, all told me, female pilots are not being judged by their gender as much as for their ability and intestinal fortitude.

There's always been, and to some extent will continue to be, a few who think women can't do some things as well as men but, I've never met a woman yet who, when she set her mind to it, couldn't do anything most men can do and maybe even better.

I made it through two tours in the Gulf of Tonkin no worse for the wear. I wasn't mindful of having been in a combat zone until after leaving the ship.

I kind of felt bad because I had it easy and the guys flying over Nam or on the ground had things much worse. For a long time I felt guilty for not doing more.

I knew I didn't deserve the Vietnam Service Medal I was now authorized to wear. Men fought and died who deserved the medal, and more, much more than me.

The Kitty Hawk was a beautiful ship when I sailed aboard her. Everything fresh and clean, the brass all polished and the paint maintained. Most certainly everyone took pride in how she looked.

I met a third class BM, *Boatswain Mate,* aboard the Kitty Hawk and he told me the difficulties to advance as a BM. However, He seemed proud of what he was doing by maintaining the ship.

It saddened me when I learned, years later, the Kitty Hawk was to be decommissioned. I saw photos of her and I guess the crew knew she wasn't going to be their home much longer and let the old girl go.

The paint wasn't maintained and rust started to appear everywhere. She began to look old and tired.

She needed much more than just a fresh coat of paint or the Navy wouldn't decommission her.

I was proud to have served on her and hoped someday Miss Kitty would be restored and made into a floating museum so others might go aboard her and see what a wonderful ship she had been.

I went aboard the USS Intrepid after she became a museum in New York harbor and I hope one day the Kitty Hawk can serve her country again in a similar way.

It's sad to think of any ship being chopped up and turned into scrap metal, such as a ship who served so proudly, been home to so many and protected our freedom and way of life for so long.

I've only seen video clips of ships sinking which is a terrible sight. The thought of having a ship, I served and lived aboard, turned into scrap is the same as seeing a ship sink.

I know sometimes better things come from scrapping the old, but it doesn't help at the time any ship goes away.

CHAPTER 9

Subic Bay

❧

Many sailors had their service time extended for a year because of Vietnam. After another cruise to the gulf of Tonkin (my second tour in the Vietnam Combat zone), I was coming up on my fifth year of service, (one year past the normal four years) and I received orders to Subic Bay Philippines to continue on to Treasure Island California for separation.

As soon as I got to Naval Station Subic Bay transit barracks, a chief approached me and asked if I would be interested in working for the MAA (Master at Arms) for the base until my transfer came through.

Having been in transit barracks several times before I knew the type of work I would be given while waiting for orders.

Assignments like galley duty, (working in the kitchen doing dishes and cleaning, not cooking), cleaning heads (bathrooms) and buffing floors in HQ or some other nasty job were common duties given to transient servicemen.

While working for the MAA I would be billeted in their barracks. I wouldn't have to stay in the transit barracks and my duties would be that of, or similar to, police work.

What he wanted for his department was a petty officer and I was a 3rd class PO. I had by that time, earned a hash mark, (a hash mark is a stripe sewn onto the lower left sleeve of your whites or blues indicating length of time in service).

In the Navy, one hash mark equals four or more years and each additional hash mark indicates four more years of service completed.

I gladly accepted the job offer and moved to the MAA barracks. The first few days I rode with a First Class or PO 1 until I learned what to do.

I got my own truck, with an old bullet type red light, and siren on top. The front facing red light oscillated and the rear facing red light just blinked. The siren was an old foot actuated, wind up, like the Indiana State Police quit using many years before.

A camper like paddy wagon mounted on the back of the pickup truck intended to be used to transport prisoners.

While on duty, I wore a white helmet liner with the letters "**MAA**" on the front and a badge and duty belt. I carried a Colt .45, model 1911, and one extra magazine as well as a nightstick.

An old two channel Motorola radio installed in the truck to stay in contact with dispatch and to talk to other units. I patrolled all areas of the base including the enlisted men's club, one of the few places I got out of the truck and walked around checking for rowdy sailors.

On infrequent occasions we went to the "O" club, (officers' club) for lunch if an officer worked the shift with us.

Sometimes three or four units got together for lunch and the officer brought us as his guests.

I was nervous at first sitting and eating with officers. We never mingled with them or became friendly with them. We didn't know if or when we might be required to arrest one of them, and we didn't like complications but the food was better and the price reasonable.

While assigned to the MAA I became quite interested in law enforcement. It would take me a while but I would in time go to the Indiana Law Enforcement Academy.

Surprisingly little trouble came from sailors at the enlisted men's club. Most of the trouble came from guys returning from liberty in Olongapo city. These problem children might be enlisted or officers.

We would take them back to their ship then turn them over to the duty officer and let them handle their own people.

Once in a while, we needed to take a violent one to the brig and the Marines loved to get them, including the officers.

One incident with a drunk Lieutenant Commander, as identified by his I.D. card, because he was in civvies.

He remained somewhat cooperative until we got him back aboard his ship. We walked up the gang way and explained the situation to the O.O.D (officer of the day), but before he could agree to take the officer aboard, the LT. Cmdr. took a poke at my partner, who just happened to be a full Commander.

I watched the guy, as my partner spoke with the O.O.D. I saw him double up his fists just before he swung at my partner's head. I grabbed the guy's arm and my partner only received a glancing blow that didn't hurt him.

We took the drunk officer to the brig and left him after telling the Marines why.

I felt sorry for that officer because I knew he would lose a rank as well as the hell he would face from the Marines.

Although I went many times, it's the only brig I've ever been in. It amazed me how clean and spit polished everything looked. Of course the prisoners did the cleaning and polished all the brass.

I couldn't believe how good it appeared. I've been in Top Brass offices before but this place put even them to shame. Not even a speck of dust could be seen anywhere and even the cracks between the tiles sparkled.

The times I'd taken prisoners into the brig, or transported them to or from the administration building for hearings and such, I always talked and joked with the Marines on duty.

When they talked to one of the prisoners, like one just being booked in, it was all business. All the Marines sounded like Drill Sergeants and it didn't make any difference what rank the prisoner.

While on road patrol one night, part of my job included traffic enforcement. I spotted a car with only one headlight illuminated. I stopped the car and walked up to the driver's door.

I saw an admiral sitting in the back seat so I popped to and saluted per protocol. I wrote the driver, a lieutenant I believe, a warning and let him go.

Several hours later I saw another vehicle with only one headlight illuminated and I made a traffic stop. I walked up to the car then realized it was the same Admiral's car.

Again, I saluted and then asked the driver when he intended to get the headlight fixed and he said he would as soon as he dropped the Admiral off at his quarters.

I let the lieutenant go when he promised to get the light fixed.

The next day, I was summoned to the legal office and a lieutenant told me an Admiral had called him that morning. He paused for effect, and then said, the Admiral told him I had done a good job on the traffic stops.

I waited for the Commander, in charge of the legal department, to come in.

He shook my hand and told me if all of his men acted as professional as I had, it would make his job a lot easier.

I felt proud of myself for doing a good job and also for being recognized as a professional. I was also happy the Admiral hadn't wanted my head.

Although I had acted professionally that night, I became aware of all my actions in the future. I was proud to be considered a professional and wanted everyone to see me in that light.

I also realized other young sailors might see me. Unconsciously I wanted to help them be as good as they could be as well.

I have always felt the desire to help others in any way possible and I think, this incident might have been the first time I ever thought about teaching.

Years later I would become an instructor at the Indiana Law Enforcement Academy. I enjoyed doing that job more than anything else I've ever done in my life. I knew some of the things the cadets learned from me could save their own and others' lives.

Law enforcement gradually crept into my blood from that point on.

Master at arms Badge
Like the first badge I ever wore.

The 1911 has been around for many years with few changes. This weapon had been issued to all services of the United States government for many years and is one of the most reliable handguns ever made. It fired a big, slow bullet, .45 caliber, which had tremendous stopping power at short range, fifty yards or less.

I won't express my opinion about the change from the .45 to the smaller 9mm other than to say those responsible were idiots although it may have paid off for them.

The 9mm weapons held more rounds than the .45, up to 15 or 18 as opposed to 8 in the .45 but the 9mm doesn't have the stopping power of the .45 bullet.

Not until I went to the MAA office did I learned how important it was to keep my weapon clean. We had to clean our rifles in boot camp but I just thought they wanted to keep us busy and learn to follow orders. After all, the Army and Marines carried rifles, not sailors.

Another incident I would like to relate; we had a dispatcher report of a stolen truck. One of the other units spotted the truck while on patrol and began to pursue the truck when it wouldn't stop.

I listened to the radio trying to figure out which way the runner might go. I heard the officer in pursuit tell dispatch the runner had hit his patrol truck.

A few seconds later, the officer, the same First Class who I had trained with, requested permission to fire on the subject to stop him. (He had hit several parked cars while fleeing). The request to fire was denied.

I found the street the fleeing truck had been reported on and waited to see if he would continue coming towards me. He did and just as he began to turn at the "T" where I waited, he lost control and struck not only my patrol truck but another car as well.

The driver of the stolen truck was apprehended and transported to the brig. A short time later, I met the First Class who had been chasing the stolen truck at the maintenance garage where I had gone to get a damaged headlight repaired.

The First Class called me over to his truck and showed me a hole in the interior of his driver's door.

I didn't need to ask what caused the hole but I did ask how he had shot his own door. He explained he had hit the door with his gun as he prepared to shoot from his open window and his gun went off. I told him he was lucky he hadn't shot his own leg or foot.

I laughed at him and he started laughing as well. I told him to use a screw driver or something and make the hole bigger and less round so no one could tell it was a bullet hole.

I found out later the kid who stole the truck had been drunk, and celebrating, because he was due to receive his discharge the next day.

He wasn't prosecuted for anything, which didn't seem right to me because an officer could've been hurt during the pursuit and he had caused quite a lot of damage. Scuttlebutt said the guy was a problem child for the Navy and the brass just wanted him gone.

As part of the MAA team, I had the same duty and liberty as they did. We had three-section duty, which means I had duty one out of every three days. This gave us two days off then one day on.

As a matter of course, our duty day lasted a full twenty-four hours, 0600 to 0600, so by the time I got off duty I was more than ready to sleep a good while.

By then I had become a heavy drinker and learned the location of all the good bars in town, Olongapo, where they took better care of us than they did regular Navy guys. To them a cop was someone to be feared and they took good care of the Pilipino cops who came in.

Most cops didn't wear uniforms but they let everyone know who they were. A lot of them carried U.S. military issue Colt .45's the same as mine but they carried them as visible as possible along with their handcuffs. We carried ours concealed if in plain clothes.

A couple of Pilipino friends invited me to a cook out one time and I loved the barbequed meat until I asked what it was: Dog. It didn't taste bad but I couldn't eat anymore.

They also had meat on a stick; cooked of course, they called monkey meat. I'm not sure if it was or not. It tasted good, a lot like beef, and I ate it quite often after that.

Another dish I ate several times while in local restaurants was called, Nadingding (The spelling may not be correct). They looked similar to green beans except they were much longer and a tad bitter but they were good.

I liked a good many local foods but don't remember what they were called. One being similar to Ramen noodle soup, or long noodle soup as I called it, which I liked very much.

I will never forget the Jeepneys in Olongapo, the city across the river, the river known by navy personnel stationed at Subic Bay as *Shit River* because of the unsanitary conditions of the water.

Originally, they converted old WWII US Army jeeps but had since been customized to open-air type vehicles used as taxies, now manufactured by several different auto makers, the most prominent being Mercedes Benz but they still resembled Jeeps hence the name Jeepney.

A couple of steps made entry up into the back of the vehicle with seating on both sides facing each other and your back to the outside. A trip from one side of town to the other side only cost locals twenty-five centavos.

One hundred centavos made one Peso and four Pesos equaled a dollar when I was stationed at Subic. A trip across town would cost about six cents American. Most of the Jeepney drivers charged sailors in uniform at least one Paso for even the shortest of rides.

Jeepneys wore bright decorations, using many colors of the rainbow, tassels and dingle danglies, funny sounding horns and Surry style tops covering the passengers.

The driver or owners used all sorts of decorations on their taxis including Bull Horns on the hood or above the windshield, bells hanging from various locations and anything else thought to give a decorative look.

Decorated as the owner/driver liked

In the background is a typical looking building of the period.

A shop or store of some kind on the ground floor and living and sleeping quarters for the family upstairs or at the back of the shop.

These mom and pop shops were most often the family's entire livelihood and little was spent on furnishings such as regular beds.

Most slept on mats or a thin mattress of some sort and a few blankets. Seldom were there any bedrooms. In fact few even had partitions of any kind. Everyone just slept in the same room, kids and parents alike.

It wasn't uncommon to see people hanging onto the outside or even sitting on top of Jeepneys. Traffic laws and laws governing safety were either non-existent or not enforced back when I was there.

At busy intersections, there might be a policeman in uniform directing traffic but still a lot of congestion remained because not everyone paid attention to the cops.

It seemed to me that accidents occurred quite often, but once the cops decided who the culpable party was the situation became rectified in short order. Depending on how much damage had been done and how much money the, at fault person, had with him or was willing to pay, the situation was often over with rather soon.

Many times the Jeepney driver just drove until someone told him to turn. It seemed he would just take everyone wherever one of the passengers wanted to go.

Most of the drivers seemed to know the city pretty well and most acted nice to service men but occasionally one tried to get much more money out of a drunken sailor or marine.

I learned to get my haircuts in town because the barber gave you a shave and scalp massage as well as a haircut for two pesos, fifty cents American.

The haircut was the usual and the scalp massage good but the shave was fantastic. Hot towels, close but gentle shaves with a straight razor, and the barber wouldn't stop until he could no longer feel any stubble.

It wasn't just service men he gave this treatment to, everyone was treated well.

Sometimes I would wait for an hour or more for my turn with only one or two men ahead of me. The wait was always worth it. Relaxing in the chair while the barber made one feel pampered.

In this shop a few shoeshine boys worked in the barbershop and most of them could make your shoes shine like mirrors.

After I found the best shine boy, I only let this one boy shine my shoes. I even brought my inspection shoes to him once. I gave him an American dollar for shining those shoes when the normal cost would only be fifty Centavos for a shine.

Pick pockets were quite prevalent in Olongapo city and most sailors in uniform back then kept their wallet either in their jumper pocket, accessed from the inside of the jumper in front, or in their back pocket of their uniform pants.

The pickpockets worked in pairs and distracted the sailor.

One of them would use a razor blade and cut the pocket so the wallet would fall out into their hand. The sailor wouldn't even realize his wallet was gone, until he needed it.

The only safe place to keep your wallet was looped over your waistband under your jumper where it couldn't be seen.

I've seen, on three different occasions, two young Pilipino guys working a sailor in uniform. When I intervened the locals would try to get me to leave but when they found out I carried a badge they left in a hurry.

While stationed at Subic Bay I learned a few words of Tagalog (pronounced, tagalo).

Tagalog is the most common dialect used in the Philippine islands but many more dialects are spoken.

Tagalog has since become the national language or dialect so in time more and more of the Philippine population will use it.

This means that people from one province may not be able to understand people from another province. I'm not positive on the spelling of any of the words I learned. *Isa baso tubig,* (one glass of water).

Other words are, *mollyit* (little), *baboy* (pig), *malaki* (big or large), *oo* (yes), *hindi* (no), *bakit* (why), *bisita* (guest), *ina iba kita* (I love you), this was said by many bar girls as they sat with a serviceman and tried to get him to buy her drinks.

Most of the girls worked for the bars and they made a small commission on each drink she sold.

They also made a little if they convinced the serviceman, their date, to buy a pass so the girl could go out of the bar she worked for and go bar hopping with the guy or whatever else they wanted to do.

I received a letter from an attorney back home saying my wife filed for divorce. The letter was postmarked while I was on the Kitty Hawk in the Gulf of Tonkin (On my second Vietnam tour).

She had stopped answering my letters and I didn't know why. I had sent several letters asking if she was alright and even sent a letter to her mother and not long after that I received the letter from her attorney.

I went to the legal office and because of my status with the MAA, a letter was fired back to her attorney, informing him I had been in a combat zone and therefore no action could be taken until I returned home.

This situation also helped speed up my orders to ship out to T.I. for separation.

I got everything packed and my sea bag ready for when my orders came down from personnel.

I liked the duty I was performing but I also wanted to get home and find out what was going on. I checked my weapon in and the rest of the gear I'd been issued.

I remained in the MAA barracks and worked the desk and radio until I got my orders. It wasn't as exciting as working the streets but still a great learning experience.

It saddened me to leave this duty. I knew I wanted to get into law enforcement. It would take a good many years before I got the chance but it came.

I think the best thing about becoming a police officer; I quit drinking. I learned a lot about how alcohol affects people and I now realize I had a major drinking problem while in the Navy and afterwards as well.

I've learned how to control my drinking now and it may take me a year or even two to drink a six pack of beer.

I still enjoy a cold beer on special occasions but I limit myself to one and only one.

CHAPTER 10

Treasure Island

❧

I GOT MY ORDERS BACK to the states. I flew back to California and went by Navy bus to Treasure Island. I believed at first many of the guys waited for discharge. I found out later most of them weren't there for discharge from the Navy.

Treasure Island or T.I., was also a large training base. They had many different schools there, one of which was electronic intelligence I believe.

I remember seeing all kinds of antennas and weird things on top of buildings. I talked to one sailor at the base and he's the one who told me they taught electronics technicians and some classes for intelligence and surveillance.

I got liberty after completing the days required duties and only needed to be back at the base for muster in the mornings. The first two days I spent a lot of time in San Francisco sightseeing. I walked to the intersection of Height and Ashbury.

For those of you who aren't old enough to remember, this is where the center of hippy culture was supposed to be located. I heard about Hippies on television but never saw any in real life until then.

Having been a clean cut sailor for five years and being raised to be respectful of others and myself, I was shocked when I walked by all the hippies.

The odor of *Marijuana* was overwhelming. I didn't know what it was at the time. The other strong smell was of unwashed bodies. The stench of B.O. seemed to hang in the air as I walked past all those people.

I saw things, I won't describe here, with regard to sexual acts right out in the open. The dress and mannerisms of the people I saw so astonished me I found myself staring at some of the people.

This was the era of free love and do as you please and it seemed everyone did their own thing without embarrassment. If it feels good do it, was the philosophy of the day.

Any direction I walked was the same, weirdly dressed men and women (those who were dressed) talking, eating, selling and buying things.

A lot of the conversations I heard were incomprehensible for the most part to me. I thought some of them were speaking another language.

Today I know they used new words to say the same things we all said or say now. They simply expressed things differently. Ya know what I mean man? I mean, are we cool chicky? Like, is everything copasetic man.

On the base I saw a doctor and a dentist, completed a lot of paperwork, and received my discharge after only three days. I got a check for my travel expenses and wages due me and cashed it at the dispersing office.

I took a cab to the bus station where I bought a ticket home. Two and a half days later, I arrived home a civilian again. The bus ride home soon became tiring sitting all the time.

My time in the U.S. Navy taught me a lot. I learned honor isn't something you learn, it's either inside you or it isn't. Courage is another thing one doesn't know he or she has until the time comes to show it.

I remember meeting an old Master Chief once, in the hanger where I worked, at Barber's Point Hawaii. I don't remember his name or his rating but I do remember how much I respected the man. He had been a Japanese prisoner of war and a survivor of the Bataan death march.

He was a quiet man when I knew him but he had served with honor and displayed courage while a prisoner of the Japanese, as did many others who were there.

I will never know all the horrors he faced then, but I know he couldn't have made it without courage and honor.

I respect and thank every veteran of all military branches of this country for their service. There's been times when I've felt I should've done more for my country. That others had done much more than I ever did while serving and many even gave all they had.

One of the advantages of talking with other vets is, one has the opportunity to learn their feelings and many say they've felt as I have. However, I've learned, and accept, not every man or woman can be a Medal of Honor winner. The part I played in the Navy was as necessary, if not as noteworthy, as what every other veteran has done or is doing.

I believe every veteran of any war trying to protect this country, our freedoms and our way of life should know one thing: many others have felt as you may.

Be it WWI, WWII, Korea, Viet Nam or any of the more recent actions involving our military men and women, you did your duty as part of the team. It isn't about what an individual vet has or has not done, but rather all of us combined, making a team effort, is what it's all about.

Even if a vet has never seen combat, he or she is still a veteran and should be proud of what they've done or do now, to serve the team, and the people of The United States of America.

I met and spoke briefly with a man wearing a WWII veteran cap the other day. He is an older fellow and walked with a slight limp. My reason for mentioning him is because of the way his face lit up when I asked about his service and thanked him.

I won't mention his last name to protect his privacy and not embarrass him.

Joe was a heavy machine gunner in Europe during the Second World War and as we spoke he seemed to appreciate being recognized as a veteran and being appreciated.

He is one of those whom I spoke of earlier having given more than me, for he was wounded over there.

I am pleased to have met and spoken with him if only for a little while. I hope we can remain in contact and I consider it an honor to call him a friend.

I think it's important for everyone, including other vets, to look for veterans and recognize them as being someone special, even walking down the isle of a store or wherever you may meet them.

Being an American Military Veteran

One who has been willing to give their life for the country they love.

One whom loved ones have missed while he or she was serving and protecting, sometimes in faraway places, and sometimes giving everything never to return.

One who has been proud to tell others they were in the service.

One who has shed tears for the loss of friends in military service.

One who has never considered him or herself a hero.

However, most importantly, it was just the right thing to do.

God Bless America

Allen W. Van Osdol Jr.

POST FACE

I am proud of my service to my country. I think everyone who isn't going into collage right after high school should go into one of the services for a couple of years at least.

I didn't realize how much growing up I needed to do until forced to take responsibility for myself.

Beginning with boot camp, I began to learn many things about being an adult I never realized.

I see young people now who are totally unaware of what it means to be responsible for anything, life is just one big party, let Mom and Dad or the government take care of everything.

There are things I am not proud of when in the Navy, my heavy drinking one of them, but overall I think I turned out to be a good sailor and citizen.

I wasn't a hero and didn't do anything special or outstanding during my time in the service, but I did serve and I tried to do the right thing, for me, my family and my country.

I've always been proud to be an American and of our countries flag.

It irks me no end to see a soiled or tattered flag being displayed. It makes me angry to the tenth degree when the American flag is desecrated in any way or by anyone, as is becoming more common in recent years.

The U.S. Navy offers so many opportunities for young men and women if they would only take advantage of them. I didn't take advantage of many things while in the Navy and wish now I had.

I encourage every reader, of military age, to look into the service of their choice and take advantage of everything you can, schooling and benefits.

While writing this book I've realized there's been much of my life I've never told anyone. I asked my Dad a few questions about his military life but he, as I, never talked much about it. The things he did share with me before he passed I appreciate and will remember.

While doing research, in preparation to tell the story of my Navy pride, I found out the base at NAS Barbers Point Hawaii has been closed and the land given to the State of Hawaii.

I also found out that both ships I served aboard, the USS Glacier and USS Kitty Hawk, have both been decommissioned.

I suppose, as the saying goes, *all good things must come to an end,* but I hoped of being able to return to visit each ship. Also some of the other places I've been to, someday, before my time here on earth is up.

I hope you enjoyed reading my story and looking at the photos I included. I did not realize how much work would be involved when I decided to tell my story but now I am glad I did for my family, friends and anyone else who enjoyed reading it.

I am a life member of the Veterans of Foreign Wars of the United States and strongly encourage every veteran who qualifies to become a member.

I've made many friends through the V.F.W. and some of them helped me deal with things that have bothered me for many years. Membership provides an opportunity for a vet to help other vets, vets who may not be as fortunate as oneself.

Another reason to belong is comradeship. Being able to talk with others with similar experiences and hearing the experiences of other vets of other conflicts. It also provides the opportunity to express gratitude for other vets contributions to our freedom. Friendships that only veterans can understand.

Being a member of any veterans organization does not mean you must be a drinker. I don't drink anywhere but at home on rare occasions now and I have several member friends who don't drink at all.

I welcome anyone who would like to contact me about becoming a member of the V.F.W. or just to have a friendly conversation. Maybe we could go to my post for a cup of coffee and swap sea stories.

Allen W. Van Osdol Jr.
Semper Fortis

DISCLAIMER

Images used in this work have been gathered from various sources: including the World Wide Web.

Authorship cannot always be credited nor the source defined.

Images credited as being borrowed from Wikimedia Commons are under one or more of the following free licenses: CC-BY, CC-BY-SA, or GFDL. Photos not given credits are either owned by the author or are in the public domain.

Every effort has been made to give proper and legal credit for all images used in this book.

I thank all who donated and allowed me to use the photographs they or a loved one has taken.

Page: 104, 105, 110, 111   Gilbert E. Brown Jr., USN Ret.
(U.S. Coast Guard, www.themaritimeguardians.com)

Page: 115   Andreyevich
(//commons.wikimedia.org/wiki/file: USS Kitty Hawk Sydney jpg)

ABOUT THE AUTHOR

Good-humoredly insightful, Allen Van Osdol's memoir, Navy Proud, provides a personal glimpse into military service and shares the life lessons a fledgling sailor learned while serving aboard the USS Kitty Hawk.

Discover what it feels like to be a veteran, and you might find yourself considering how you can serve your community, too.

www.ingramcontent.com/pod-product-compliance
Lightning Source LLC
Chambersburg PA
CBHW060254050426
42448CB00009B/1636